If you really want to help your heartbroken friend . . .

> *"Right after Bruce died, for two or three weeks I just sat in a chair down in the family room and stared at the clock on the wall,"* Martha explained. *"Sometimes I would sit there for twelve hours.*
>
> *"It got so bad that eventually I couldn't even get out to go to the doctor. When I was so far gone in self-pity and depression, I would think:* I need help, somebody. I need somebody to help me. *But there was absolutely no way I could call and ask for it."*

If you really want to help your heartbroken friend, you'll have to find a way to convince her: Your problem is *our* problem. When you're weak, I'll help you stand. If you fall, I'll help you up again.

Making God Visible

How to Help Your Heartbroken Friend

DAVID B. BIEBEL, DMin

MAKING GOD VISIBLE: How to Help Your Heartbroken Friend
Copyright © 2016 by David B. Biebel

Published by:
Healthy Life Press • 6700 Wadsworth Blvd., Apt. 101 • Arvada, CO 80003
www.healthylifepress.com

Author: David B. Biebel, DMin
Designer: Judy Johnson
Cover Photo: © Pakhnyushchyy | Dreamstime.com

Printed in the United States of America

No part of this publication may be reproduced, stored in a retrieval system, or transmitted in any form or by any means—for example, electronic, photocopy, recording—without the prior written permission of the author, except for brief quotations in printed reviews.

Library of Congress Cataloging-in-Publication Data
Biebel, David B.
Making God Visible: How to Help Your Heartbroken Friend

ISBN 978-1-939267-23-8
1. Caring – Religious aspects – Christianity;
2. Helping behavior – Religious aspects – Christianity;
3. Friendship – Religious aspects – Christianity.

Unless otherwise identified, Scripture quotations are from the HOLY BIBLE, NEW INTERNATIONAL VERSION®. Copyright © 1973,1978,1984 by International Bible Society. Used by permission of Zondervan Bible Publishing House. All rights reserved.

NKJV is from the NEW KING JAMES VERSION of the Bible. Copyright© 1979, 1980, 1982, Thomas Nelson, Inc., Publishers.

NASB denotes the New American Standard Bible. Copyright © 1960, 1962, 1963, 1968, 1971, 1972, 1973, 1975, 1977, 1995 by The Lockman Foundation. All rights reserved.

Capitalization of pronouns related to deity follows *The Christian Writer's Manual of Style* (Grand Rapids: Zondervan, 2004). In biblical quotes, capitalization of pronouns related to deity follows the translation in use.

Most Healthy life Press resources are available wherever books are sold. Distribution is primarily through *Amazon.com, deepershopping.com*, and *healthylifepress.com*. Multiple copy discounts available directly from Healthy Life Press. Wholesale distribution is through *springarbor.com* (a division of *IngramContent.com*), and *deepershopping.com*. Our ePublications are available through *healthylifepress.com, Amazon.com* (Kindle), *BN.com* (Nook), and for all eBook readers through *deepershopping.com*. Wholesale pricing is available through *IngramContent.com* (*springarbor.com*).

This book is a revised and updated version of *How to Help a Heartbroken Friend*, by the same author.

Contents

Foreword

Author's Note

1.	What to say when you don't know what to say	1
2.	A loneliness that must be shared	17
3.	An emptiness that must be filled	35
4.	Healing the wounds on their own terms	49
5.	Becoming your friend's soul-mate	65
6.	Life goes on	79
7.	What to do when you don't know what to do	95
8.	Somebody to hold me	113
9.	To tell the truth	131
10.	Moving with the pain	147
11.	Beauty for ashes	163
12.	Seven habits of highly effective comforters	173

Notes	195
About the Author	196
More From This Author	197
Resources from Healthy Life Press	198

The Spirit of the Sovereign Lord is on me,
  because the Lord has anointed me
  to proclaim good news to the poor.
He has sent me to bind up the brokenhearted,
  to proclaim freedom for the captives
  and release from darkness for the prisoners,
to proclaim the year of the Lord's favor
  and the day of vengeance of our God,
to comfort all who mourn . . .
to bestow on them a crown of beauty
  instead of ashes,
the oil of gladness
  instead of mourning,
and a garment of praise
  instead of a spirit of despair.
They will be called oaks of righteousness,
  a planting of the Lord
  for the display of his splendor.

They will rebuild the ancient ruins
  and restore the places long devastated;
they will renew the ruined cities
  that have been devastated for generations.

~ Isaiah 61:1-4

Author's Note

Even though this book is written in the first person, many of its ideas and insights were not original with me, but grew out of the interaction of the study group that helped develop and polish the principles. Except for anecdotes that are autobiographical, I have disguised the identities of the group members along with certain facts in their stories to protect their privacy. Other material is from letters I've received from the scores of surveys returned to me by brokenhearted people. Their names are disguised also, and some details are altered to protect their privacy. Unless otherwise indicated or obvious from the text, however, the illustrations are based on the true experiences of people who know about heartbreak and its physical, relational, psychic, and spiritual pain. To each of them, I wish a personalized overflowing portion of God's grace.

P.S. I have struggled with the question of gender-neutral language, and decided that instead of using s/he or they, them, etc., I will alternate he and she throughout the text, as long as it doesn't detract from the flow, or confuse the frame of reference.

Chapter 1

What to say when you don't know what to say

Sometimes nothing is best.

After three years of faithful service to an aerospace corporation, Marty lost his job. He went to work one day and, in between the classes he was teaching, he heard the rumor. Two weeks later it was confirmed by a terse note that sent the forty-seven-year-old human relations expert reeling: *We regret that due to an unforeseen downturn in our markets worldwide, your position has been terminated.*

The initial shock was tough enough. Worse, though, was that after four months of trying everywhere and everyone he knew, Marty still had no job. Not even a prospect of a job. What had started as a challenge had slowly ground away his confidence and self-respect to the point where life seemed pointless and he even considered suicide as a solution.

Finally, one day, the frustration and fears got the best of him. Alone in his apartment, Marty started shouting at God, "Why did you do this to me? What did I do to deserve this? Don't you care what happens to me?" The heartbroken man carried on for some time, venting his anger, screaming and pounding on things.

After there were no more tears to cry, he noticed his dog, Mandy, cowering behind the living room chair, a witness to the whole thing. "Come here, pup," Marty said quietly, as he sat down to recover his composure. "You should be glad you're a dog. At least you can't get fired from being man's best friend." Then Marty explained to Mandy just how tough things had become lately.

When he was done, he took the dog out for a walk, partly to be sure nobody else in the condo had overheard the tantrum. Thankfully, nobody had—or if so, they didn't let on. Relieved at this, Marty was even more relieved to have gotten the bitterness out of his system.

You might think the relief came from all the things he said to God, and certainly that was part of it. But Mandy played a big part, too. Unlike some of Marty's human friends, his faithful dog didn't argue or offer solutions or advice. She just listened, wagging her tail and licking her master's hand once in a while to let him know she cared.

Let's face it. Life hurts. Sometimes it hurts so bad it seems that nothing could ease the pain, much less heal the wound causing the distress. This is as true for Bible-believing, church-going, born-again people as it is for everybody else. In fact, your brokenhearted Christian friends may have it worse, because, like Marty, they have to deal with whatever loss has occurred while wondering, "Where was God when I needed him?"

Before you rush to offer a dispassionate, logical, or even theological answer to this question, remember Mandy. If you rush to fix what's broken—broken *hearts* are the ultimate challenge—you may miss the point completely. Marty simply needed somebody to hear him out, a sounding board, someone willing to enter his pain and share it with him. When the crisis came to a head, Mandy's compassionate presence was more comforting to Marty than all the suggestions made by his pastor and church friends, who seemed either unable to understand or unwilling to authenticate his suffering.

The reason I begin with Marty's story—instead of one of the more horrific tales you'll hear about shortly—is to illustrate something crucial about heartbreak. The intensity of Marty's grief had more to do with his background and personality than with the relative magnitude of his loss. The human "help" he had received was meaningless, at best, and infuriating, at worst, because it failed to connect with Marty uniquely, individually, right where he was, without judging him for being there and without telling him how he should feel or what he should do to get out.

> *Let's face it. Life hurts. Sometimes it hurts so bad it seems that nothing could ease the pain, much less heal the wound causing the distress.*

So a good question is: If Jesus were there, how would he have tried to help Marty?

The Continuum

Now let's go to your church together, you and I, and try to identify the brokenhearted people in the pews around us. They're not usually easy to find, because they arrived all prissied up and bravely masked to match everybody else. But look into their eyes, observe the stress in their faces and the tension in their frames. If your church allows opportunities for people to express themselves, listen to the meaning—really, a yearning—hidden in what they ask or say. It's a simple longing: *Won't somebody please just be my friend?*

You may not be able to pick up these vibes without some practice. But for the sake of the 30 percent (my estimate may be much too low) of the people around you in any church service who fit this category, I hope you won't give up too easily.

Contrary to what you may believe, you don't have to endure some disaster before you can bring a touch of God's grace to a heartbroken friend. If I might rephrase the apostle Paul: "Shall we hurt the more that grace may the more abound? May it never be!" In 2 Corinthians 1, Paul reminds us that we've all had pain of some kind, and with God's help we can comfort others with the same kind of comfort we received from him.

Comfort, like pain, is a continuum. It's true that widows understand widows, but it's not true that you have to be a widow to help one of them toward wholeness. In fact, sometimes a potential comforter's previous loss may hinder her ability to really help a heartbroken friend, if the helper has not yet resolved her own issues. When this is true, the helper may try to work out her own pain through the other person, which is neither fair nor helpful because while the "comforter" may feel better as a result, the heartbroken person will end up more confused.

But anyone willing to walk in a heartbroken friend's shoes for a while can be helpful, even if her greatest tragedy to date was getting dumped for somebody else as an adolescent. You can make all the difference in a friend's healing.

Lonely Even in a Crowd

Our hypothetical church service has gotten beyond the announcements, hymns, special music, and the offering, but you still haven't zeroed in on anybody who seems to exhibit more than normal distress. So we might as well listen to what the guest speaker is saying. "Listen, grump," he says. "You know what your problem is? It's your attitude! Life has its problems. We all know that. Nobody said it would be easy, but why all the doom and gloom? Everybody falls into a pit once in a while, but you don't have to wallow in it, throwing a pity party nobody wants to attend. We're not pigs . . . we're eagles, who on wings of faith can rise above anything and everything the devil throws our way.

"Did you wake up this morning with a chip on your shoulder? Then get back in that bed and get out on the other side! Happiness is a choice, after all. If you're depressed, it's because you *want* to be depressed. Maybe you even *like* to be depressed. If you can't see the bright side of life, it's because you don't *want* to. There's no other logical—or spiritual— reason.

"You've got to take off those melancholy spectacles and look at life with positive eyes of faith! God gave you two eyes for a reason. Some people gaze at their problem with both eyes and never look at God. Some gaze at the problem with one eye and glance at God with the other. Some glance at the problem with one eye and gaze at God with the other. But the only way to live the victorious life is to gaze at God with both eyes, and never give those little problems the slightest glance."

As the people applaud, and the preacher launches into another entertaining story to support his point, you notice that Nancy, just to your right and one pew forward—almost within reach—is weeping silently, with a slightly bowed head.

You might be surprised to know that the most alone she ever feels is when she's in church. If you earn the right to get inside her pain, you'll find out why.

Nancy attends your church every week, not out of obligation or as a social event, and certainly not to be entertained. She keeps coming because in her heart of hearts she is still a little girl who believes that her heavenly Father loves her more than she dares to ask or think. That child-like faith kept her sane when her older brother tortured her by leaving her on a blanket under which numerous mouse traps had been set. Her caring Father was there in her hiding place, a hollow in the stream bank behind her home. And when she began splitting into different personalities to mentally escape the more extreme abuses that came later, he loved each "person" in a slightly different way.

When Nancy goes to church, she sees—and is frightened by—the mass of people. She hears about all the programs and plans, and like everyone else she stands up and sits down on cue. She gives what she can, and she tries to stay open to the sermons, although the one she's hearing right now and others like it only add to her overwhelming sense of shame, while increasing her fear that nobody really understands or cares. She told me once she's been to a lot of churches, but almost everywhere she goes she feels like an alien, disconnected from everybody else.

More than anything, Nancy desperately needs—and wants—to stay in touch with the ever-healing Spirit of God. She needs to know that God is now here, as opposed to "God is nowhere," which she is sometimes tempted to believe.

The good news is, you can help. The bad news is, getting involved with her will cost you—time, energy, but mostly love. She doesn't need another program, even a small group program. She's endured a lot of them already. She doesn't need a psychiatrist. She's seen dozens of them already, and one has made himself available by phone, anytime.

What Nancy really needs is a friend. **One will do.**

People Can Say the Stupidest Things

Nancy's sense of disconnection may be more extreme than most, but it's one of heartbreak's common themes.

Nearly all our group members struggled with this, sometimes by choice but more often because of an interchange like the following, adapted from a role-play in which Katherine has come "to comfort" Martha, a new widow:

K: I don't have to pick up the kids for twenty minutes, so I just thought I would stop in and comfort you, like Jesus said.

M: I'm so glad you came over. I just feel so isolated, and so—

K: But honey, Jesus is with you.

M: I know Jesus is with me.

K: He said he'll never leave us. Your husband left you, but Jesus said that he'll never leave you.

M: Well, I still was feeling really lonely, and I apprec—

K: (Interrupting) I know just how you feel. This happened to my mother-in-law. When her first husband died, she was just beside herself. We didn't know what to do with her. But then she started going to another church and she met this nice widower. I'm sure that the Lord in his time will bring you another mate.

M: I'm really not interested in another mate.

K: She said the very same thing!

M: Do you really think there's something wrong with me that I'm feeling lost and lonely? I know Jesus is here with me and I find comfort in the Scriptures, but I still miss my husband.

K: Oh, Martha, but he's in heaven. He wouldn't want to come back here, even for ten minutes, because he's with the Lord. You wouldn't want to wish him back in this wicked world.

M: Well, what about me?

K: Now I've never lost a husband, but I know that time takes care of things like this.

M: How can you know that if you've never experienced it?

K: I just read the Word. I just believe what God says.

M: (to herself: *Haven't you ever read the book of Job?*) I appreciate your coming, and I appreciate what you've had to say, and I welcome company anytime. I'll see if there's something wrong with me that I feel the way I do.

K: Well, you just keep praying. And call me anytime, I'm happy to come over and be God's comfort.

M: Any time I need your comfort, I'll call. . . .

It'll be a hot day at the North Pole before Martha calls Katherine. But Katherine will probably expect that call. Not only that, she may be offended not to hear from Martha, now that she's gone out of her way to minister to Martha's need. To top it off, she may even chastise Martha, probably in the church foyer or parking lot, for not calling, and for the way she has withdrawn from people, when a lot of women have had it worse than her.

Actually, in this role play, Martha was far more confrontational with Katherine than most heartbroken people dare, or care, to be, either because they don't have the energy or because they're too emotionally numb to get angry. If there's anything that comes through loud and clear from my research into this question, it's this:

For some reason people who want to help often aren't wise enough to say nothing when they don't know what to say.

The Sounds of Silence

Perhaps to defend God's honor, or to try to make some sense of what has happened or simply to put the whole thing in the past, most would-be comforters are convinced that *something must be said*. That was Marty's experience, when what he really needed was somebody to let him unload. In other words, his friends might have communicated more by not saying anything.

When the eleven-year-old brother of one of our group members died, after the funeral and the reception and just about the time everybody was leaving, the pastor showed up at her family's home. He took a seat in the living room and sat there for a couple of hours, listening, observing, just being around. After the well-wishers had left, he still stayed for a while. Then he talked a little with the family, prayed with them and left. The net impact: *Dallas came. Dallas was here.*

That was what they remembered after the flowers wilted and the hoopla died away.

Being there is more important than almost anything else.

I learned this myself in the spring of 1979, sitting on the bank of a small pond in the little town in Michigan's Upper Peninsula where I was the only pastor. A young boy had drowned, and as I sat with his mother on that hillside waiting for the diver to find the boy's body, I didn't know what to say, so I didn't say much.

But this brokenhearted mother knew I cared, and maybe she thought I understood, having buried my own three-year-old son, Jonathan, the previous fall. As we waited, being there was all I could offer. Sometimes it's the best and only way to deal with a hurt that pious words of consolation might only magnify.

Since you're reading this book, it's clear you want to sharpen your comforting skills. Speaking for all the people I've heard from through the years: Thank you! You *can* learn to listen. You *really can help* your heartbroken friend, if you will do just one thing, truly. Love her.

Love, No Wax

Perhaps you've heard 1 Corinthians 13 called the "Love Chapter" of the Bible. But did you realize that the apostle Paul penned those beautiful words to a group of believers who had been so marvelously blessed with divine gifts that they sometimes forgot to express them in love?

"The most excellent way" of love calls believers beyond spectacular manifestations of the Spirit—prophecy, knowledge, and supernatural faith—beyond extreme generosity and even martyrdom, to a redemptive personal involvement with each other. For love is patient, kind, not envious, boastful, or proud. It isn't rude or self-seeking, isn't easily provoked nor does it keep a record of wrongs. It rejoices with truth, protects, trusts, hopes, and always perseveres. And when it has these characteristics, love never fails.

Although this book is not intended as an indictment of anyone, the sad fact is that (except in rare churches) the ability to love in this way has been lost in the fast-paced, superficial experience we call "faith." It would be misleading, therefore, to let you pass this page without making it clear that *really loving your heartbroken friend may put your own faith to the ultimate test.*

In New Testament days, dishonest pottery dealers would try to salvage damaged pieces of their finest, and thinnest, wares by rubbing wax into the cracks and then setting those pieces in the shadows in hopes a gullible buyer would purchase them. Discerning shoppers would take these items out into the light and hold them up to the sun, which easily displayed even a hairline fracture. Pottery that passed the test was "sun-tested," because it was "without wax." The word *sincere* comes from these two root words.

The only really helpful thing you have to offer a heartbroken friend is love. This book is about more than insights into the grieving process and strategies to help. At its most fundamental level, it is about finding ways to love your friends from their brokenhearted fragmentation—regardless of its cause—toward a new sense of wholeness, through linking you and them, by faith, to the healing love of God.

It's one thing to say you love somebody. But it's an entirely different matter when, having heard your words, your hurting friend holds you up to the sun—metaphorically, of course—to see if the love you offer is really as sincere as it appears to be.

In the following chapters, you'll find many practical suggestions about how to demonstrate the reality of your love. My hope is that you'll benefit from our group's collective experience with grief—both positive and negative—and gain from our losses. Most of all I hope you'll discover how the many facets of love can match and meet the highly individualized needs of your heartbroken friends. You can make a real difference.

For Reflection or Discussion

1. If you are studying this in a group setting, ask each person to share what she or he hopes to gain from the course, and why.

2. Ask two volunteers to role-play a brief conversation between Marty (the unemployed man in the first story) and one of his Christian friends. When complete, choose the two or three best points each party made. Ask "Marty" what things helped and what didn't, and note these in your "practical list of dos and don'ts"—a continuing chalkboard exercise through the entire study. Print out a list for each group member at the end.

3. What does it mean to *individualize your caring?*

4. Is the estimate that 30 percent of people in church on a given Sunday morning are struggling with a broken heart

too high, too low, about right? Can you offer any evidence to back up your own estimate, or is it mostly intuitive?

5. In your own experience, is the hypothetical sermon in the text typical, atypical, or highly unlikely in today's church? If you've ever heard a sermon like this, what was your reaction at the time? If positive, or at least neutral, did you wonder how some members of the congregation might be taking it?

6. While Nancy's case is rare, stories like hers are surfacing much too often these days. How could you try to meet Nancy's need of friendship without putting her privacy in this extremely delicate matter at risk?

7. What's your response to the question of what to say when you don't know what to say?
    - ❏ All things work together for good.
    - ❏ Into each life some rain must fall.
    - ❏ I'm sorry.
    - ❏ I don't know what to say, but I do love you.
    - ❏ Nothing at all.
    - ❏ Is this a trick question?

8. How could Katherine have been more helpful to Martha? After discussing this, replay this conversation with more sensitivity, if you have time.

9. In 1 Corinthians 8:1, the apostle Paul says, "Knowledge puffs up, but love builds up." Yet when we try to help heartbroken people, we often give them knowledge: facts, ideas, concepts, principles. Why?

- ❏ Truth is the only way beyond the pain.
- ❏ Their minds have to control their emotions through knowledge.
- ❏ It keeps them at arm's length and I don't really want to invest the energy and time to get involved.
- ❏ If they don't take good advice, it's their problem.
- ❏ I couldn't mail myself, so I sent a card instead.

10. Have someone read 1 Corinthians 13:4-8a with the goal of identifying which aspects of love described there fit each illustration in chapter one.

11. Complete this statement: In order to really help my heartbroken friend, I need to. . . .

Share your answers as a group, and pray that in the coming weeks you will become even more effective comforters than you are now. You will. God will honor your desire.

Chapter 2

A loneliness that must be shared

Be the rare source of real comfort.

Sometimes it's nearly impossible for heartbroken people to believe that there really is a way beyond their pain. But you can break through and give that hope, if you'll be as sensitive and creative as Martha was when she and Katherine reversed roles in our group. Here's an adapted version of how the visit went:

> M: Katherine, I've been thinking about you a lot and wondering how you're doing. Would this be a good time to visit for a little while?
>
> K: Oh, come on in, Martha. I won't be much company, but I'm glad to see you.
>
> M: You don't have to be company, I just want to be with you.
>
> K: Thank you.
>
> M: How are you doing, really?

K: Oh, it depends on who I talk to. When I'm at church and someone asks how I am, without stopping, I just say "fine." But I'm really not doing very well. Martha, what am I going to do?

M: I don't know. I wish I had all the answers. But I do know there are a lot of people who care about you and a lot of people who want to be here for you. And I know you'll make it through, even if I can't tell you how.

K: Everybody thinks I'm so strong, but I don't know what to do. Jeremy's only ten. Heather's only eight. What am I going to do? Doug . . . gosh, he was funny. And I'm not funny.

M: What do you miss most about him?

K: His laughter. He was the kids' favorite. God took the wrong parent.

M: Well, I can understand you saying that, but you're special to the children in your own way.

K: I don't know, the only thing they'll ever remember about me is my saying, "Don't make a mess."

M: What do you most want them to remember about Doug?

K: The fact that he laughed and he prayed. But they aren't going to remember that, they're so little.

M: Maybe you can help them. Could you capture any of it, so that when they're older they'll remember?

K: Maybe just by talking about him. After Doug's mother died, his dad wouldn't let us talk about her, and I don't want my kids feeling like that.

M: Anything else? What would help you remember him? What sparks memories of him right now?

K: Being able to talk about him, without having somebody say "Don't feel that way."

M: You're a talented writer. Maybe it's too soon but sometime you could write some stories about the family, all of you together, so the kids would have them to read and to remember him by. It might be good for you, too.

K: I hadn't thought about that. You know the other night, though—this is really going to sound stupid—I really wanted to talk to Doug. When I started writing my mom a letter, I ended up writing to him instead. Am I crazy?

M: No, you're not crazy at all. I think that's a very healthy thing for you to do.

K: Really?

M: Really. I think it's beautiful. And I hope you kept it.

K: I did, 'cause I couldn't mail it.

Role-playing Reality

The reason Martha was so helpful in this case was that she remembered how desperately she had needed a friend after her own husband died. "Right after Bruce died," she explained, "for two or three weeks I just sat in a chair down in the family room and stared at the clock on the wall.

"Sometimes I would sit there for twelve hours, doing noth-

> "So I prayed, 'God, if you're there, send somebody to help me, because I'm desperate and I can't do anything to get myself out of this.'"

ing but that. But I had two little kids, and I had a horrible battle going on inside me: *I have to do something, but I can't, I just can't. I can't even lift my hand; I can't do anything. But I have to do something.*

"It got so bad that eventually I couldn't even get out and go to the doctor. I called him, instead, and he prescribed a tranquilizer to elevate me from depression. But what it did was really zonk me, so then I could hardly stay awake.

"When I was so far gone in self-pity and depression I would think: *I need help, somebody, I need somebody to help me.* But there was absolutely no way I could call and ask for it.

"So I prayed, 'God, if you're there, send somebody to help me, because I'm desperate and I can't do anything to get myself out of this.'"

Loneliness is one of grief's most devastating outcomes. If you really want to help your heartbroken friend, you'll have to find a way to intercept her retreat to the only safe place left—inside herself. You'll have to find a way to convince her: Your problem is *our* problem. When you're weak, I'll help you stand. If you fall, I'll help you up again.

Unfortunately, comforting of this ilk is a rare commodity, especially among Christians. For some reason, the church is an army that shoots its wounded.

Purple Heartless Club

Frank and Rose Williams were both high-profile leaders in their assembly, anxious to hear the group's shared wisdom when Rose found her "dream house" and wondered if buying it would be God's will. A combination of circumstances, including finding a buyer for their current house, seemed to indicate they should.

After a great deal of prayer and encouragement by their friends, they took the plunge. But after Rose and Frank moved into the new house, their buyer backed out, and suddenly they had a serious financial crisis instead of proof positive that God was involved.

"The 'friends' who confirmed God's will to us when everything was going well now will have nothing to do with us," Rose wrote. "Our church has provided almost no support. My family doesn't understand. And I have been shaken to the core. I have gone all the way back to the beginning in my relationship with God. What does he really promise us?

"This has been the most painful experience of my life."

In some churches, where "faith" means agreement with the current pastor's interpretation of Scripture, people are not often prepared to get down and get dirty when disaster strikes a fellow member. The sermons over the past year have focused on principles of positive faith, every service ending with a gospel presentation and an altar call for salvation, rededication, or in some groups, an invitation to receive the "baptism of the Spirit."

The problem is not so much with any of these components —but with limiting what we call "church" to activities held in a certain building during certain time periods of the week, following a certain format led by certain trained professionals.

In New Testament times, early Christians shared all things in common, including their joys and sorrows. The Greek word for this shared life is *koinonia*, from the root *koinos*, which means "common." An almost identical word, *koinonos*, means "partaker" or "partner." Beyond the transforming message of new life through faith in Jesus, the most revolutionary thing those early believers offered was: *One with him means one with us. From now on, we're in this* ***together***.

These Greek words are sometimes translated "fellowship," which in many churches today is *something you do* in a place called the "fellowship hall," where it is highly unlikely a heartbroken person is going to rain on everybody else's parade by telling the truth about how much life hurts. Perhaps it is in the nature of institutions that protocol, programs, and progress gain higher priority than participating in someone else's pain.

But I have to believe the latter can happen without threatening the former in any way. In fact, *the more people become partners in life, the more they will want to become partners in faith*. But if conformity to some autocratic leader's way of seeing or doing things is all they share, both their faith and their ability to help their heartbroken friends will be deficient, and their "comforting" will degenerate into a rather sanctimonious form of abuse.

"Our church pastor made things *worse*," Rose said. "He accused us of not giving enough and of having unconfessed sin in our lives. After fourteen months, we couldn't take it anymore. We found a small church where, ironically, many others have come after being hurt at other churches. Having to leave a church that was our home for nine years, and knowing that most people didn't understand why we had to go, is the thing that still hurts the most, even after two and a half years."

Making a Diagnosis

I'm not indicting this fellow, since I've failed enough parishioners myself. For example, Sandra's battle with multiple sclerosis began when I was her pastor. Here's how she remembers my response: "[You] had serious personal problems and said, 'You will have to find someone else to talk to. I can't be your pastor.'

"There was no one else," she continued. "There never has been."

Naturally, I don't recall saying those words, but I do remember being absorbed by my own grief after Jonathan's death. And I do recall not knowing how to help Sandra. At least I didn't condemn her, except to the intense loneliness she described.

So instead of blaming anybody, let's view this as a diagnosis: We could be much better at bearing one another's burdens, thus fulfilling the law of Christ—the law of love. Yet, sometimes we can't even seem to fulfill the "Golden Rule."

Why should a pastor's wife, just returned from burying her dearly beloved twenty-eight-year-old daughter—killed by a drunken driver—have to endure this statement, her very first Sunday after the funeral? "I told her not to ride that motorcycle or she'd be killed."

Why should her husband have to endure this question from another of their parishioners: "Did you go to that young man in jail and put your arm around him and tell him you loved him and forgave him?"

When the pastor said, "No, I didn't," the fellow added insult to injury when he responded, "Well, I'll pray for you until you do."

How can it happen so consistently that we who claim to know, worship, and emulate the One who fulfilled the prophecy, "A bruised reed he will not break, and a smoldering wick he will not snuff out" (Matt. 12:20) can be so insensitive toward the pain of people we're supposed to care about? After giving this a lot of thought, I think it really comes down to faulty spiritual wiring.

This same pastor now looks back in amazement at the teaching he endorsed before his daughter's death. "I used to hear a lot of preachers and other people say 'once you become a Christian, you won't have any more problems.' I always preached that when those valleys and hard times come, God will come in a great way and you'll just be on top of the world and walk right on through with a smile on your face.

"Then we learned that good people do suffer and go through the dark night of the soul, wondering if God is there and hears them."

Identifying the Causes

One reason Job's story is so timeless is because the issues he grappled with are still common to brokenhearted people today. I'm not speaking only of the spiritual agony of feeling abandoned by God, but the emotional, physical, and relational pain that came from losing first his wealth, his children, and then his health, followed by his human support system, beginning with his wife, who suggested he might as well curse God and die.

Job's relational pain intensified, however, when his three friends—Eliphaz, Bildad, and Zophar—began to attack him for trying to express a heartbreak that nearly defied words:

> Why did I not perish at birth. . . ?
> For now I would be lying down in peace; . . .

> Why is light given to those in misery, and life to the bitter of soul, to those who long for death that does not come, who search for it more than for hidden treasure, who are filled with gladness and rejoice when they reach the grave?
> Why is life given to a man whose way is hidden, whom God has hedged in?
> (Job 3:11,13, 20-22)

Eliphaz summarizes the earliest version of what continues to be the self-righteous approach to the brokenhearted:

> But who can keep from speaking?
> Think how you have instructed many, how you have strengthened feeble hands . . . [and] faltering knees.
> But now trouble comes to you, and you are discouraged; it strikes you, and you are dismayed.
> Should not your piety be your confidence and your blameless ways your hope?
> Consider now: Who, being innocent, has ever perished?
> Where were the upright ever destroyed?
> As I have observed, those who plow evil and those who sow trouble reap it . . .
> Blessed is the man whom God corrects; so do not despise the discipline of the Almighty.
> For he wounds, but he also binds up; he injures, but his hands also heal . . .
> We have examined this, and it is true.
> So hear it and apply it to yourself.
> (Job 4:2-8,5:17-18,27)

Job, now one of the loneliest men who ever lived, replies:

> A despairing man should have the devotion of his friends, even though he forsakes the fear of the Almighty.
> But my brothers are as undependable as intermittent streams; . . .
> Now you too have proved to be of no help; you see something dreadful and are afraid . . .
> Do you mean to correct what I say, and treat the words of a despairing man as wind?
> You would even cast lots for the fatherless and barter away your friend.
>
> (Job 6:14-15, 21, 26-27)

Back and forth they went, Job's "comforters" condemning him while their former mentor and role model maintained his integrity, justifying himself and occasionally challenging God.

Job's affliction had created the same problem for both Job and his friends. Their belief system, which he had probably taught them—good things happen to good people and bad things happen to bad people—might not be trustworthy.

What so "terrified" Job's comforters was this train of thought: *Job has tried with all his heart and soul to walk uprightly before God. If such calamity has come upon him, what's to keep something even worse from happening to* us?

Unwilling to let their categories expand to embrace both Job's realities and God's character—too much paradox and ambiguity for such rigid folks!—they chose the only option left: They rejected the very person they had come to comfort.

Needed—Listeners

When you commit yourself to helping heartbroken friends, be aware that the further you get inside their loss, the more uncomfortable you may feel, and not just because of the intensity of *their* feelings. Your discomfort comes because what has happened to them does not mesh very well with your understanding of who God is and how he works in our world.

But take the risk, please, not only for the sake of your friends, who desperately need someone to share their loneliness. You will benefit, too, by sharing the journey, because it will expand your own circle of love while it stretches your faith.

Your main concern, especially if this helping role is new to you, should be learning to listen. Listen, listen, listen. There's no better way to pierce the loneliness of heartbreak.

Interestingly enough, this rare ability is not primarily a passive exercise in which you function as a human tape recorder. Therapeutic listening involves learning *how to ask the right questions*, including feedback responses intended to clarify and encourage your friend to keep going deeper. In this process, she may discover—to her surprise—*what she really thinks or feels* about whatever issue you're helping her process at the time. Several of our group members commented on the importance of having someone who can help you understand what's really going on. One, a bereaved mother with a handicapped son said, "Sometimes your feelings are pouring out and it's not very coherent. I wasn't a sorter. I was just dumping. But it really helped to have my counselor give me a list of emotions or feedback like, 'Okay, this is what you're saying.' He might restate it wrong, but I could always respond, 'No, I don't mean that.'"

Another woman needed someone to coax her feelings out, because no one had ever modeled for her how to express what was inside. "I needed someone to listen to what I was *thinking*," she said, "somebody to read my mind. In my family, you didn't talk about anything. My mother had a breakdown when I was in junior high, and to this day, I don't know what caused it. All I remember is she cried every day, and I couldn't help her, couldn't get to her.

"So, you didn't talk about those things. I needed somebody to pull it out of me. I didn't need somebody to say, 'I'm going to listen to your heartache,' because I wouldn't know where to start."

Obviously, people differ in their ability to verbalize their hurts, so you'll need wisdom to be able to discern how to individualize your listening style to match their need. But here are some guiding principles that will fit many situations:

- Make sure you are there, with them, and not somewhere else, even if you've heard this story ten times before. One impatient glance at your watch, or a vacant stare when you've just been asked a question, and you'll have to work very hard to recover their trust.

- One way to stay there is to maintain eye contact and a posture that indicates you really do want to hear what's being said. Lean toward the speaker, and touch when appropriate.

- Give feedback instead of advice. Ask leading questions instead of making statements. For instance, you might follow an angry outburst with, "You sound upset . . . please help me understand how you feel."

- But if you say, "If you don't deal with that bitterness this minute, you can't expect God to heal you," you may get compliance without heart, which isn't real and therefore isn't worth pursuing.

- Don't react judgmentally, regardless of what your friend says. This may be a test, to see whether you're more committed to loving your friend than to defending God's reputation.

- Never say, "I know exactly how you feel," followed by a lengthy discourse on your own heartbreaks. Your own hurts may have equipped you to understand, and at some point it may be useful to let the other person know you've traveled a similar path. But always keep in mind that your highest priority is *the healthy completion of your* friend's *journey*.

- Finally, remember, no matter how much you may wish you could help your friends recover, their problems are their problems, regardless of how far they let you inside their loneliness. In the end, they alone can choose to pursue whatever decisions or directions seem best.

In this helping relationship, you can become redemptively involved in answering Rose's question about what God really promises. If there is any single theme resounding through both Old and New Testaments in relation to heartbreak it is this: "Do not fear, for I am with you."

But it can be nearly impossible for a heartbroken person to believe this until someone like you comes alongside to, as one of my friends said, "Make God visible."

For Reflection or Discussion

1. What did you think about Katherine's writing a letter to her deceased husband?
   - ❏ Weird. The ultimate denial.
   - ❏ Beautiful. She probably needed to express her love to him.
   - ❏ Futile. What difference does it make?
   - ❏ Great idea. I think I'll do the same in relation to somebody who's gone on before me, to whom I wish I said some things.
2. If a lot of heartbroken people sit in their family rooms staring at the clock for twelve hours at a time, as Martha did, how can we help them?
3. If you knew someone was praying: "God, if you're there, send somebody to help me because I'm desperate and I can't do anything to get myself out of this," what would you do about it?
4. Draw a picture of loneliness, and then in a group setting, have group members (as many as wish to) show their sketches. What are the common themes? Try to create a composite group sketch of what loneliness looks like.
5. In your experience (personally or by observation), is the church an army that shoots its wounded? Give examples if you agree with this sentiment. Also, brainstorm some solutions to this problem.
6. Have you ever gone ahead with something, believing it was God's will, only to run into multiple problems, as Rose and Frank did? Share these experiences briefly, the

personal and theological questions raised, and finally how a caring friend might have helped when the crisis was at its worst.

7. Rose admitted she was shaken to the core, and that she went all the way back to the beginning in her relationship with God. Why do you think she reacted so strongly?
    - ❏ She was just a big baby; after all, she owned two houses when some people never get to own even one.
    - ❏ She had bought into a false system, including its idea of who God is and how he works in the world.
    - ❏ She felt abandoned by everyone she thought cared about her.
    - ❏ She wasn't well enough versed in positive thinking.

8. What's more important in your own church: protocol, programs, progress, or people's problems? Prioritize the list as you think God sees things.

9. Do you think it is true that the more people become partners in life, the more they will want to become partners in faith?
    - ❏ Sounds a little New-Agey to me.
    - ❏ Puts the cart before the horse. Gospel is first, life second.
    - ❏ I don't understand what "partners in life" means.
    - ❏ It's about time we stopped separating these.

10. Could you understand why Rose said, "Having to leave a church that was our home for nine years . . . hurts the most"?

    Try to decide as a group which losses hurt Rose the

most and why: ostracized by friends, condemned by friends, misunderstood by friends, ignored by friends.

11. If you were the pastor whose daughter had been killed by the drunk driver, how would you have reacted to the parishioner's question: "Did you go to that young man in jail and put your arm around him and tell him you loved him and that you forgave him?"

    Why might people feel obligated to say such things?

12. Have two group members role-play the first interchange of Job and Eliphaz in a modem context based on Job 3:1-7:21.

    Why do you think Job's friends reacted as they did? Are any of their reactions still common today?

13. Job complained that his "brothers were as undependable as intermittent streams." Is there a modem way to express this dilemma that compounds the pain of our fellow travelers?

14. Do good things happen to good people and bad things happen to bad people?

15. Create your own list of emotions with a view toward helping your heartbroken friend accurately label how she feels.

16. Once you've created this list, role-play a conversation between the bereaved mother and her counselor.

17. Share any insights you may have in terms of how to reassure your friend, through your involvement, that God's promise to be with her is true.

    Pray that the Lord would show you creative ways to communicate this truth to heartbroken people in your church. He will.

Chapter 3

An emptiness that must be filled

Fill it with yourself.

Christine was abused beyond what most of us can imagine. "I lost my childhood," she wrote. "At the age of twenty-eight I began remembering things that confirmed that as a child I was physically and sexually abused in very violent ways by my parents and the satanic cult they were involved in. When I got into therapy, I discovered that all the blank spots throughout my childhood were my way of wiping away the ugly stuff."

A lot of people draw a blank when they remember their childhood. Sometimes it's only with the help of a skilled counselor that they are able to fill in what happened. They then realize that the unconscious source of what's been driving them for as long as they can recall is an *intense inner search to fill a void* they can't even define. But they do know this: *Something's missing*.

Of course, it's nearly impossible for disinterested observers to offer much real help to someone like Christine, although that doesn't necessarily keep them from offering advice. People didn't understand the depth of my pain," she said, "but they still offered advice like, 'You just need to have a better self-image.' Yeah, right, like I can bake it up in the oven and suddenly, poof, out comes a wonderful self-image. Give me a break, please. I'd like to see others go through what I have and come out with a rosy self-image."

I Had Everything, but Was Empty Inside

Even affluence can create a vacuum like this. Misty grew up in a very materialistic, upper middle-class family, surrounded by everything she ever wanted or needed, from clothes to cars, except one thing: nurturing love.

In her case, emotional deprivation was the norm, combined with a lot of pressure to look good and perform well. Once she was left, at six, at a fashion show where *she was the emcee*, the night her mother gave birth to her sister.

Her father, a salesman, was never home. Her mother, although there physically, was very unstable. The only communication she recalls was, "Clean your room."

When Misty was nineteen her parents divorced, which further devastated the little girl inside the now-grown woman's body who still longed for some kind of relationship with her parents.

When everything seemed to be falling apart Mindy held together because she had become a Christian and was attending a Christian college in her hometown. Also, without realizing why, she had begun latching on to older women in a desperate effort to find the mother's love she'd never known.

This went on until Misty was twenty-four, still searching

for somebody to tuck her into bed at night. Finally, she found Stacy, a woman with a family of her own who was willing to love Misty unconditionally and commit to being her friend, whatever it took, until Misty's emotional wounds were healed.

Stacy, acting on the advice of Misty's counselor, tried to create for the younger woman the childhood things she'd missed. She tucked Misty into bed with words the young woman had never heard, but will never forget, "Good night, love."

Such tender moments had their down side, however, because Misty grew to hate herself for needing them. "I started causing problems in the relationship because it was good," Misty recalls, "and I didn't know how to deal with *good*. I could deal with turmoil, so if there wasn't turmoil, I created it."

In other words, regardless of how desperate Misty was to fill an inner vacuum that she described as a bottomless pit, in one part of herself she needed the emptiness because it was the only thing she had ever known. This is the reason children of alcoholics marry alcoholics, or victims of various abuses keep going back to their abusers. It may feel bad to feel bad, but at least there's some security in it.

Stacy and Misty went through a lot together over seven years, but one of the most helpful things Stacy did for her younger friend was to teach her how to nurture and sustain herself.

For instance, nobody had ever rocked Misty, so Stacy gave her a rocking chair, and taught her to rock herself, to visualize Stacy rocking her, or her own mother rocking her. Now Misty's house is full of rocking chairs.

"She also helped me visualize a healing place, the place where I wanted to go," Misty said, "because I got so frustrated with how long my healing was taking. *She* could see the changes, but the increments were so small *I* couldn't see them myself. In order to illustrate where I was headed, she read me that childhood story about the moonflower that blossoms at night. She told me I would know when I was healed, and she would know it, too. And she promised to give me that story as a milestone when the day finally came. Shortly after I moved to Colorado, a package arrived from Stacy. It was the moonflower story, written out in longhand."

Creative Nurturing

Not everyone has an internal void as significant as Misty's or Christine's, yet their journeys illustrate how competent adults (they both were serving with Christian ministries) can conceal a need that only good friends can meet.

Counselors are helpful, yes, especially in the initial stages of discovering where the holes are. But the long-term healing for emptiness like this takes a far deeper involvement in a person's life than any counselor is able to fulfill. Misty's story is about how an untrained woman who cared became the frontline helper while the counselors became the support team as time went on.

We live in such a specialized society that when someone like Christine or Misty comes into our lives, instead of really trying to help them, we refer them as quickly as possible to some professional. But, as one of my psychiatrist friends reminded me, before there were psychiatrists, there were friends.

You can help the Christine's or Misty's that you already know—you might be surprised how many there are—but to do it you'll have to be willing to pay the kind of price their inner healing will require of you.

They don't know how to fill the hole themselves. Somebody has to fill it for them, then *with* them, and then show them how to fill it themselves. Ideas won't do it. Principles, techniques, and advice may help, but only a *person* can fill the kind of hole we're talking about, because only a person has the flexibility to discern the uniqueness of each individual's inner need and then create a personalized, healing balm to match it.

Occasionally, as Stacy discovered, the one who is trying to help must personally take the place of what is missing, at least until the brokenhearted friend has received what was lost (or never even offered). When this happens, you will be fulfilling a role like that of the Old Testament "scapegoat," upon whose head was placed the sins of the people on the Day of Atonement, and who was driven into the wilderness afterward.

This symbolized Jesus' role on the cross, when he voluntarily took upon himself the sins of all who would believe in him, and then entered the wilderness of abandonment when he said, "My God, my God, why have you forsaken me?" (Mark 15:34). When you choose to take upon yourself the heartbreak of another to this degree, you are becoming as much like Jesus as you will ever be. But don't be surprised how much it hurts. Caring costs. There's no way around it. Yet, in the end, the joy of seeing your heartbroken friend healed will far outweigh any of your expenses in the process. Stacy would certainly agree with that.

Laughing on the Outside, But . . .

Unfortunately, sometimes children are forced into this scapegoat role by their parents, and when this happens another kind of internal vacancy occurs.

Jeremy's father was a livestock wrangler in Hollywood. If there was a stampede, he was the one who created it, then rounded up the cattle while the cameras were still rolling. His mother, on the other hand, seemed "to live in a constant state of emotional trauma," he said. "To this day, trouble just seems to seek her out. She lives a turbulent life; there's never any peace."

Jeremy, who was one of our group members, still battles with some of the issues bequeathed to him by his parents. His mother, apparently working with his dad, had a horse fall on her, crushing one of her legs. By the time bad had turned to worse, her body was reacting to the steel pin in her leg, and she ended up a drug addict through the opium-derivative medication she received for her pain.

> Little Jeremy's problem was that his parents were so busy fighting, there was never anybody there for him—no one to talk to or share with. No one to fill the emptiness inside.

"Sometime in this whole scenario," he told us, "my mom and dad got into a real bad argument, and Mom went out to a bar where she got drunk, and the bartender took advantage of her, raped her, and made her pregnant. She tried to abort this baby by riding roller coasters and horses and giving her body a generally hard time, but nothing worked. And in the middle of it all, my father left us."

After the baby was born and given to another family to raise, Jeremy's father returned, but now he was abusive, beating his wife and his children with whips. The sad result was that this little boy became his mother's main support system.

"We didn't have anything," Jeremy recalls. "We moved to the backwoods of Texas into a little house with two rooms and no furniture, except a table that was made out of a door and a couple of sawhorses. Strange as it sounds, though, I had a horse. I remember riding that horse when I was really little, playing Lone Ranger. But then one December my mother asked me if I was willing to sell my horse so we could have a Christmas."

Little Jeremy's problem was that his parents were so busy fighting, there was never anybody there for him—no one to talk to or share with. No one to fill the emptiness inside.

So to fill a void that must be filled, Jeremy turned to sex, primarily because when he was a boy one of his male cousins had been sexually abusive toward him, lighting a fire of lust that turned into an addiction before he became an adult.

"I was always looking for someone to be there for me," he said, "but I didn't even know what that meant. I didn't understand. You walk out into the cruel world and you say, 'Whoa! Where am I? Now what do I do?'"

Jeremy enlisted in the military because he figured it would teach him discipline, but all he learned in the Air Force was how to circumvent the system. The only good result was that his assignment brought him to Las Vegas, where he met his future wife, Toni, then a patient in a psychiatric hospital, when he went to visit *her roommate*.

Here was an opportunity to fulfill the only role in which Jeremy was comfortable—saving the failing female. To make a very long story short, they're doing well today, but they've had their moments of playing the "I'm your father, you're my mother" game. "We fought like nobody I'd ever seen," he said.

"I remember being on top of the car with Toni trying to run me over. Or I'd lock her in the bedroom and just listen to her scream until she busted through a window . . . dumb stuff like that."

Even though Jeremy was internalizing stress he didn't deserve, and trying to fill a hole he didn't understand, on the outside he described himself as, "A funny guy, a barrel of laughs to be around. But nobody knew who I was. *I didn't know who I was.*"

Jeremy, the funny guy, was a living example of Proverbs 14:13, "Even in laughter the heart may ache, and joy may end in grief."

One of his most poignant comments was, "It was only after I became a Christian that I wanted to kill myself, put a gun to my head; because then I began to see the truth and I couldn't handle it. I could pretend, block it out, fake it, but I couldn't handle the truth when I started learning a lot of things about myself."

The Helper's Dilemma

Here's the problem, in bold print. Starting to learn things about yourself begins with finding a friend willing to help you separate truth from fantasy. But sorting out the truth can be excruciatingly painful for people like Christine, Misty, or Jeremy, because maintaining the fantasy feels so much better.

Beyond the resistance—even antagonism—that may arise when you try to help somebody like this, working with them can tap unconscious fears in yourself, because all of us have some kind of hole we're desperately trying to fill.

Here are some suggestions if you decide to embrace the extreme needs heartbroken people like these may present:

- Take *every* suicidal comment seriously. Don't pretend you didn't hear. Instead, say something like this: "I can understand how you might want to escape from all of this, but I care very much about you and I want you to live. So if you insist on talking like this, I'll have no other choice but to take you seriously and call someone to protect you from yourself. Now tell me, how serious are you?"
- Don't fill your friend's void with nothing, specifically, words, concepts (including theological concepts), or platitudes. His need is far more complicated than that. Only a person can meet it, starting with you, but ultimately leading to another, even more able Person, who understands what it means to feel abandoned.
- Realize that the reason you want to withdraw (if you do) is because the need your friend is expressing is either way beyond what you think you can handle or in an area that you would rather leave undisturbed in your own psyche. Face the truth squarely—and move on.
- Be patient. Blamers who have been scapegoats need to tell their story over and over and over again. Look for an opportunity to short-circuit the cycle, once you have proven your loyalty, by saying: "I've heard you describe this before. Can we stop for just a moment and talk about it?"
- Be ready to become a scapegoat yourself, specifically, to take the emotional pain upon your own "head," so this person can move beyond bondage to it. While this is happening, be sure you have your own partner to support you in prayer.
- But, even with your prayer partner, never divulge the other person's secrets. People with "holes" often dump

a lot of garbage. But if you reveal confidences and this becomes known to the person you are trying to help, you may *never be able to recover that same level of trust.*

- Try to discover not only what the person's inner vacuum is, and how it happened, but how to creatively fill it.

Here is the way Stacy tried to do this for Misty, once she realized what Misty's needs really were. Stacy gave her younger friend "Misty's Love Alphabet," written out, one letter at a time, on the pages of a sticky pad:

A: Misty is authentic. (Not phoney)
B: Misty is beautiful. (Not only physically)
C: Misty is comforting. (Reaches out to hurting people)
D: Misty is deep. (She looks for more than superficial characteristics)
E: Misty is energetic. (Loads a fast dishwasher)
F: Misty is fervent. (Intensely devoted)
G: Misty is generous. (Gives out of love)
H: Misty is home-loving. (Loves the qualities of home)
I: Misty is insightful. (Sees with more than eyes)
J: Misty is just. (Sees fairness in all things)
K: Misty is kind. (Not mean)
L: Misty is lovable. (Easy to love)
M: Misty is a mother's delight. (I'm proud of her)
N: Misty is needed. (She's important to me)
O: Misty is outstanding. (No ordinary girl here!)
P: Misty is poised. (She handles different situations with aplomb)

Q: Misty is quality. (Knows good stuff and is good stuff)
R: Misty is responsible. (Always dependable)
S: Misty is spunky. (Spirited, plucky)
T: Misty is trustworthy. (She can be trusted to do it, keep it, say it)
U: Misty is understanding. (Perceptive, fine-tuned)
V: Misty is valued highly. (By many, mainly Stacy)
W: Misty is wonderful. (Amazing, remarkable, very fine)
X: Misty is X-tra. (Out of the ordinary)
Y: Misty says yes. (She is open to receive love from many)
Z: Misty has zest. (Keen pleasure in living and loving)

Through Spirit-driven creativity like this, even something as common as a sticky-pad can become a life-transforming epistle to fill a love-starved soul, another very creative example of how we can make God visible to our friends who are brokenhearted.

If you know someone who struggles to fill an emptiness he or she has entrusted to you, ask the Lord to show you how to start.

For Reflection or Discussion

1. When Christine began to fill in what was missing in her childhood—through the help of a qualified counselor—she discovered some truly sinister memories. It is possible that by reading her story, you have been reminded of

something similar. If so, how do you plan to process this pain? What help could a friend be in this journey? Do you have the professional support you need?

2. Do you agree that emotional deprivation creates the same kind of inner vacuum as ritual sexual abuse? Defend your position.
3. Have you ever had a friend like Stacy? Describe how that person helped fill some void in your life.
4. Recall the way your mother (or father) tucked you into bed with words like, "Good night, love." How is this reflected in the way you perceive God's love for you today?
5. Discuss the implications of this statement: "Before there were psychiatrists, there were friends."
6. Have you ever witnessed anybody playing the "I'm your father, I'm your mother game"? Describe the dynamics without violating anybody's privacy. If several members of your group feel strongly enough about this, have volunteers create a role-play on this theme.
7. Have you ever personally been somebody's scapegoat, either by his choice or yours? Describe the feelings involved.
    Is there some redemptive use for this role today? If so, how can a person embrace it for the good of another?
8. Have you known anyone who was laughing on the outside but crying on the inside? If you got through the facade, what did you discover that person's real issue was?
9. Identify some common "platitudes" that amount to "filling your friend's void with nothing."
10. Start to create a love alphabet for Jeremy, based on what

you know about his story. If there is someone you are working with now who has an emptiness like what this chapter discusses, find a simple way to give a gift such as this, and watch what happens.

Chapter 4

Healing the wounds on their own terms

They won't heal any other way.

For fifteen years Buffy was Gary's best friend. Gary's parents and grandparents had all died by the time he was twenty-one, and he had no brothers or sisters. Gary never married either, so Buffy, his horse, filled a huge need in the middle-aged fellow's life.

Suddenly, however, Buffy got very sick and had to be put to sleep. As a result, Gary had what he called a "mental breakdown" because he had loved his horse so deeply. The hurt was so great, Gary didn't have the heart to love any other person or animal. He wasn't suicidal or bitter; just tired. He felt totally useless and was convinced there was no point in his staying alive. Every day, he prayed that God would let him die. When this failed, he wondered if he was being punished. Convinced that he would never know lasting peace or happiness in this world, he wanted to go to a place where these things would become reality.

Gary's psychologist speculated that he was experiencing delayed grieving in relation to all the losses in his life. Gary tried to agree, but for him the real grief was being left behind. He simply wanted to be where his family and pets were.

The clergy he consulted scoffed at the idea that his pets were in heaven, but he couldn't imagine heaven without them. After all, he figured, God made animals before humans, and Jesus talked about the value to God of even a little sparrow.

Evidently, Gary's heartbreak was an anomaly to his would-be comforters. The psychologist wanted to theorize it away, and the ministers wanted to theologize it away, but Gary's problem remained—how do I find a way to embrace living when all my friends have died?

By phone and by letter, I tried to address both sides of this heartbroken person's need. Theologically (or intellectually) I told him I thought there was more evidence than not in the Bible for animals in heaven, or shall we say when God has made the new heavens and the new earth, where people and animals will all be friends again. But, I added, I also expect that the glory of God and the wonder of being with him will so far outweigh the other joys (our reunion with those who have gone before, whether human or not) that they will seem pale by comparison. The problem, we will then know (as C.S. Lewis wrote), is not that we loved the others too much, but that we loved God not enough.

Gary's real problem was that his heart had been broken—again—and he was afraid to allow himself to love anyone, or anything—again. Behind all that was a heart full of love, so as I recall, I suggested that he get involved with an animal shelter where there would be many animals with an unlimited need for what he had to give.

Gary's professional comforters had tried (rather unsuccessfully, as far as I could see) to help him beyond his heartbreak, by forcing his reaction through their framework (psychological and/or religious) instead of authenticating his reaction by engaging his heartbreak on its own terms (and turf). Gary needed to hear, both verbally and non-verbally, "It's only normal to mourn the loss of a close friend—and Buffy was the best friend you had. The degree of your hurt is related to how deeply you cared for him."

Answering Questions Nobody's Asking

I've been on both sides of this issue myself. I've preached funeral sermons with a "salvation" message and even an invitation *when nobody was asking, "How can I be saved?"* I've sat through two funeral sermons over my three-year-old son Jonathan (we had two services) that addressed a lot of issues, but not the ones that haunted me: "If this is what we get for serving God, what's the use, anyway?" or "How can I love and serve a God who either causes or allows such things to happen?"

Even in my counseling, I would listen to clients describe their situations and then tell them *what I'd been through and how I'd handled it*, when what they needed was not another load on top of theirs, but someone to say, "You've really been through a lot; would you help me understand how it feels?"

If you're really going to help your heartbroken friends, you'll have to meet them in the center of their own pain and convince them to let you walk with them through it to the other side. Informing them what their issues are—because these are the ones you're most familiar and comfortable with—and where they must head in order to resolve their hurt *may actually seem to help them in the short run*. The hurting person may say the right things and do the right things, and have every appearance of doing well when, for example, the

> *Denial is a boomerang that always comes back to hit somebody in the face.*

pastor makes a post-funeral visit. But after he leaves with a positive feeling about where the person is headed, only a few months later he, along with everyone else in the church, is totally surprised when that same person goes over the edge, one way or another. Denial is a boomerang that always comes back to hit somebody in the face.

Dealing with heartbreak in *any* prepackaged way *cannot really help* in the long-term (otherwise known as real life) because sooner or later heartbroken persons realize that the answers they've embraced and acted upon had nothing to do with their real questions, still unresolved.

If or when this happens, it may usher in this potentially detrimental, but logical, sequence of thought: "When my heart was broken, nobody would hear me out. Instead, they pressured me to accept answers to questions *they thought I should be asking* instead of the ones *I really wanted to ask*. But now it's clear that their best answers don't fit my real questions, so I'll just find my answers somewhere else."

Rushing Things Just Makes It Longer

As you may recall from the previous chapter, Jeremy met his future wife, Toni, when she was a patient in a psychiatric hospital. Toni was hospitalized after one of her numerous suicide attempts, her way of trying to escape the heartbreak of her adolescence, when her father sexually abused her for years, until he made her pregnant at age sixteen.

Jeremy, already well-trained by his mother as a rescuer, spent the first few years of their marriage trying to rescue Toni. "I'm a good example of what not to do," Jeremy admitted. "Most times when this poor woman was trying to share something with me, I just wanted to fix it. 'You know, you should do this' and so forth. My tendency was to say, 'Okay, now what do we do to get beyond this? Let's get out the Bondo, patch this puppy up, and get on down the road.'"

"Jeremy never meant to hurt me by asking 'What are we going to do to get over this?'" Toni replied. "But I was supposed to jump right into his solution and I wasn't ready for that. I really needed to bellyache for about six years."

Nobody else wanted to hear it, either. "Sympathy, to me, has always been a thumbs down," Toni said. "I'd tell people everything that was bothering me and they would treat me like, 'What do you want, sympathy?' or 'How many years ago did you say that was?'

"I'm in the depths of despair and I'm so weak and no one can pull me out of it. All they can say is 'Toughen up!' Well, I'm not ready to toughen up. I'll be tough when I'm good and ready."

If your heartbroken friend had a dollar for every time he's heard, "Don't you think you should be over it by now?" he could take you on a trip to Disney World. The problem is, until he is over it, he won't care to go along himself.

Although there is no divinely inspired timetable for various types of loss, most people seem to have one. My heartbroken friends who returned surveys often mentioned how impatient and unkind people could be. Here are a few choice remarks I hope you'll never make:

- *You're too depressed to be around.* "This was three months after Timothy was stillborn," a young woman wrote. "A pastor-friend believed Scripture says we should not grieve and that God is disappointed with us and our hardness of heart if we do."

- *Well, I guess it's all over now.* A man said this to a woman about three weeks after the funeral of her seven-year-old. "My own mother made comments like that when at four weeks I was depressed somewhat," she added.
- *When are you going to get rid of that wheelchair?* "As if I could make up my mind and get well," wrote a woman with multiple sclerosis. "But the classic came from an older lady: 'When you first came to our church, it seemed you would be such an asset. And now you are one of those people who is always needing something!'"

A missionary summed up the kind of patient involvement required if you really are going to meet your friend's heartbreak on its own terms. This woman struggled with a "destructive addiction," from which the only logical escape she could see was suicide: "People expressed impatience or dissatisfaction with me—whose own agenda for my recovery was more important—but their expectations hindered my waiting on the Lord. Many people are oblivious to their own weaknesses and avoid getting into situations that are difficult to handle. When they see others struggling, some become judgmental or critical.

"We get uncomfortable with someone else who is trying, and instead of rejoicing in truth, get angry at having our own weakness exposed. Being brokenhearted involves facing one's own weaknesses, sins, limitations. For people to be empathetic, they have to be willing to become brokenhearted [with you]. Not many are willing to enter into such brokenness."

Time Alone Heals Nothing

Some people say that time heals. But some wounds only love can heal—love over a long period of time. God made us all different—intellectually, temperamentally, spiritually, not to mention male and female; and we've all been influenced by culture (education, media, role models) and subculture (family, church, peer group) in relation to handling heartbreak. Because of this, no two people, including spouses who love each other deeply, can respond identically to a mutually devastating event, either in terms of how long recovering takes or what methods they use to cope with the pain.

If there is anything that surprises heartbroken couples (as well as their friends) it is this: Heartbreak is a better wedge than it is a glue. Depending on the circumstances, marriage partners may be thrown together initially by the sheer force of a loss. But unless they work very hard at understanding and helping one another process the feelings unique to each, they will begin at some point to diverge in their pilgrimage with pain. If your heartbroken friend is married, this is one of the factors you will need to keep in mind if you're going to help.

Here's the way it was for several members of our group: "Dan and I reacted quite differently to our daughter's death, right from the beginning," Mary said. "He took the early morning call, and when I heard him say, 'Not my Minny!' I knew I didn't want to hear it. He wanted to be held, but I couldn't stand to be held. I just threw back the covers and said, 'I have to do something.'

"I don't even remember what I did, but I had to be busy. I thought that a husband and wife would be together, but it seemed from that moment Dan went one way and I went another. He became a couch potato, and I rushed around, ninety miles an hour. He wanted to take a vacation, and I couldn't stand to because it would be too much time to think.

"Instead, I walked. I walked miles and miles. I cleaned the house, cleaned the car, and I overdid everything, but you do anything you can, just to survive. I bounced off every wall in the place. The person I had invested my life in was gone. My faith went out the window. God just seemed like he was a long way away."

By contrast, Dan, a pastor for thirty years, said, "Mary suffered with grief a long time. She carries it more. I've tried to analyze why we're so different, and I think it goes way back to when I was nine and my mother died. The way I coped with that then is the way I still cope with grief today: If I don't think about it, the pain goes away."

"Why have you been so sick?" Mary interjected.

"Probably because I held it inside. But I don't know another way," Dan replied.

"We talked about putting on our happy faces when we went to church," Mary continued, "but I noticed that Dan started spending more and more hours in front of the TV, alone. He became a recluse."

"I think I withdrew because I was disappointed in the parishioners' reactions," Dan said. "I guess I hoped that when I came home from the funeral, things would be a little bit easier, that maybe they'd let up their relentless attack.

But it didn't happen. So I just didn't want to be around people. I could get up, go to church, and preach, but as soon as church was over, I'd just go home, close the door, and pull the curtains."

I could identify with Dan's experience. After Jonathan died, I still had to preach, teach, evangelize, counsel, and visit—all on an emotionally empty tank. I'd drag myself out of the slough of despond (which in my case was filled with the quicksand of guilt) just far enough to carry out my Sunday duties before sliding into the muck again by Monday morning. I knew some of my parishioners cared, and they tried to help us. But there were enough of the others who disapproved of my depression and were anxious for me to get back into the pastoral saddle as if nothing had happened, which added even more guilt to my already unwieldy load.

I'll never forget how I tried, in one deacon's meeting, to express my inadequacy and fears. I just couldn't force myself out the door, midweek, to do the visitation that was expected. I needed help, and I was asking for it from them. But instead of figuring out how they could share this burden with me (which I believed, and still do, was as much their responsibility as mine), one old-timer settled the matter by saying, "The people are waiting for the pastor to visit."

One thing was sure for me: I needed a new venue. So within a few months, the venue changed, but the path continued. Five years after moving to a para-church ministry, our second son Christopher was stricken with the same rare, genetically linked, brain-damaging illness that had killed Jonathan. This time, I took the road more traveled than many would care to admit. Desperate for something, anything to dull the pain, if only for a moment, I found myself attracted to another woman, partly because the one I'd lived with for seventeen years was now so consumed by her own grief that she had little interest in meeting my needs.

We had become strangers on the *via dolorosa*—the way of suffering. Only by God's grace did I manage to stay faithful. (Christopher, by the way, survived and has done very well.)

How to Minister to Your Minister

Just in case the heartbroken person you're trying to help is your pastor, I have a few suggestions, all aimed at overcoming Dan's summary of his journey with heartbreak: "There was no one there for me."

Pastors may seem way up there somewhere, and you may feel you can't really understand. But I promise you: *You don't have to understand your pastor, as long your pastor understands that you care.*

<u>Don't:</u>
- Re-preach one of his sermons or quote Romans 8:28.
- Judge him—he feels bad enough already.
- Tell him he should be over this already.
- Remind him that people are watching, so he should be a good example.
- Pray *for* him (in the sense that it's *his* problem).

<u>Do:</u>
- Allow him to be human—he is, you know. Allow him to express his emotions, and accept him when he does.
- Love him; put your arm around him.
- Take him golfing (or fishing or whatever you used to do together).
- Give him time, as much as he needs.
- Pray *with* him (in the sense that it's *our* problem).

In doing these things, you'll be acting like Jesus, mending

a bruised reed and renewing a smoldering wick so that others will be blessed when this person's ability to minister is restored. In other words, you'll be making God visible.

To use another analogy, I planted an orchard in New Hampshire and enjoyed seeing how those small fruit trees began to grow. Sometimes their small trunks would become damaged, perhaps nicked by a mower. If I noticed it soon enough, and bound that wounded bark back in place, the tree could heal itself. But if I waited too long, and the wound became diseased or dried out, that little tree might be in danger of not surviving long enough to ever produce fruit.

This same kind of binding up can be applied to broken hearts, but timing is essential and care is a must. So before you go to try to accomplish this, pray *for yourself*, something like this:

> Lord, help me be discerning enough to understand what's happening with my friend, wise enough to speak the right words at the right time, and sensitive enough to do so in a therapeutic way. Help me discard perceptions and expectations that arise from a purely human point of view and utilize, instead, the insight that only your Spirit can give. My friend needs help, Lord, and I believe you want me to try to provide it. But I am afraid, afraid of my inadequacy to share this hurt in a way that will take us both toward wholeness. So I entrust us both into your grace, believing you will help me help my heartbroken friend. Amen.

For Reflection or Discussion

1. Have a group member with a deep affection for one of his or her pets play the role of Gary, whose horse, Buffy, has died. Have two other members play the parts of the counselor and the pastor, respectively, each in his or her professional office.

    Debrief following these interchanges, asking each role player to share his or her reaction, followed by the group's perception of what has taken place. Try, especially, to answer these questions: Was Gary's depression legitimate? How would you try to help him?

2. What happens to a helping relationship when the helper forces the other person's issues through his or her own framework? If this has happened to you personally, share its result.

3. Discuss the difference between "dealing with" a person's heartbreak and "entering his pain," in order to understand and share it.

4. In your experience, have you been the recipient of answers to questions you weren't asking? Describe this encounter to the group, and see if you can suggest another approach that might have been more helpful.

5. Review and discuss the "choice remarks I hope you'll never make." If you have made comments like these when trying to help a heartbroken friend, see if you can develop a different way to express yourself.

6. Jeremy was constantly trying to fix Toni, who needed something else from him. Ask a couple of volunteers to role play this typical male-female difference in the following case:

The female was kidnapped six months ago, held for ransom, and threatened with sexual assault, but rescued before this actually took place. She still has nightmares, especially since the trial is now underway, but her husband seems more relieved that she is home safe and he would prefer to put this all behind them and get on with life.

7. How do you react when you hear that missionaries sometimes have "destructive addictions"?
   - ❏ Not surprised—they're human.
   - ❏ Worried—that my support may be funding something like that.
   - ❏ Depressed—if it happens to them, it can happen to me.
   - ❏ Disappointed—that all our heroes turn out to have clay feet.

8. What do you think would happen to this woman's financial base if the details of her very difficult struggle became public?

   Suppose this missionary, home on furlough, has come to stay with you and she confides that her addiction was sexual and she's worried that the temptations will return when she returns to Germany. How would you try to help her?

9. If your heartbroken friend says that the way he handles loss is not to think about it, so the pain goes away, is it better to accept this or to force him to talk about it?

10. In Luke 7:31-35, Jesus puts an intriguing message in the mouths of marketplace children: "We played the flute for you, and you did not dance; we sang a dirge and you did

not cry." Examine the larger context, then discuss the lesson here in terms of responding appropriately to different situations:

- ❑ Market goers can be a pretty mellow group.
- ❑ Stereotypes don't fit when it comes to Jesus.
- ❑ Some people can't express extreme emotions.
- ❑ There's no "religiously correct" approach to joy or sorrow.
- ❑ Followers of Jesus should feel free to fully experience life's joys and sorrows.

11. The apostle Paul put it another way: "Rejoice with those who rejoice; mourn with those who mourn" (Rom. 12:15). Which of these is more difficult, and why? How can we learn to share life more fully with our friends?

Chapter 5

Becoming your friend's soul mate

We'll survive this—and we'll do it together.

One October day in 1989, Jenny's twenty-one-year-old daughter, Angie, was talking with her boyfriend about their future. It wasn't really an argument, but in the middle of it she got up and walked into another room (with him following), picked up his handgun, swung it around, and it went off. The police recorded Angie's death as an accidental self-inflicted gunshot wound, since there was no depression, no suicidal ideation, no clues. Nobody will ever know if it was intentional or not.

"As you know," Jenny wrote to me, "Christians can be less than kind and this is a superb gossip opportunity. If one more person says 'read your Bible and pray, dear,' I may become unkind myself."

At first people visited and called, sent cards, and brought food. This was especially helpful, because Jenny's husband and their five other children still needed to eat. It was all Jenny could do to heat up what had been provided, but nearly impossible for her to function well enough to carry on her normal routine.

What kept Jenny sane was a professional counselor who allowed her to yell in anger at God about the unfairness of it all. The counselor also taught her enough coping skills to survive the journey, including exercise, relaxation techniques, visualization techniques, blocking, remembering that others also hurt, taking parenting one day at a time, journaling, and personal two- to three-day retreats. The only coping strategy that connected her directly with another person, however, was to "call someone." In other words, if she wanted help, *she had to ask for it*, a very difficult thing for a devastated person to do until the only other option is jumping off a high bridge with a short rope around your neck. Heartbreak is a lonely road.

What made it worse was Jenny's feeling that everybody, including God, had turned their back on her. "Friends and acquaintances literally walked away," Jenny wrote, "crossed the street, turned around in a store aisle, quickly walked past me, and so on.

> But the real kicker occurred when a letter arrived from her own brother, a minister, saying, "I can't absolve her; you'll have to accept that she's probably in hell."

"I expected they would be there for us and let us hurt," Jenny says. "I know they do care, but simply have no understanding of how to demonstrate that. Love is not enough; it has to be love with action. Love enough to carry a piece of my pain as they share my hurt. The church was our major social life, so our social structure fell apart. We were just plain ignored by most of our church, judged by some. I really struggle with the realization that my non-Christian friends have been much more *there* than my Christian friends. Why?"

One friend leveled with her, at least, "You guys have been through so much [a whole series of crises] and you always thanked God through it all, smiling along the way. You're crying now and we don't know what to do with you."

Well, Jenny noted, "I don't know what to do with me either!"

Her pastor didn't visit until a month after the funeral, and when he did, he said, "I have trouble dealing with death." But the real kicker occurred when a letter arrived from her own brother, a minister, saying, "I can't absolve her; you'll have to accept that she's probably in hell."

By contrast, a person with no theological axe to grind might hug Jenny, and after using some expletive to describe her trouble, say, "Fate is fate, but friends are friends. If we don't help each other, nobody else will."

Here Come da' Judge

The comments I've received from disappointed people like Jenny are frightfully consistent in terms of how their Christian friends have not only failed to help them, but added to their hurt by their misguided "comfort."

Through the years, I've identified four styles of "comforting," the first two of which are detrimental, the third neutral, and the fourth the only one that really helps: the critic/judge; the advice-giver; the identifier; the soul mate. Let's examine each of these and their effects, because many would-be helpers have not given their helping styles enough thought, including how *the way they're trying to help may be hindering their friend's progress toward wholeness.*

For the sake of visualizing this, let's say your friend, Charlie, has fallen into a pit filled with slime which is threatening to pull him under. If he works at it, even a little, he can keep his head (or at least his nose) barely out of the sludge. If he gives up, he'll slide under and drown, a temptation that increases with time because the longer he treads muck the more exhausted he becomes. Charlie cannot climb out because the sides are too steep and slippery. If he is going to survive, he needs help.

Along comes the critic/judge, who, upon seeing Charlie in the pit, polishes his halo, grabs his Bible, and loudly recites five reasons why people fall into pits. The more self-righteous the orator, the more personalized will be the judgment pronounced. In general, it sounds like this: "People fall into pits because they have sin in their lives. But, if you will yet repent, perhaps the Lord will rescue you."

When our first son, Jonathan, became ill, several of the younger men in the church speculated that God let this happen because I was too materialistic. After Jonathan died, I confessed to a local Christian physician that I thought I had loved him more than anything, perhaps maybe more than I loved God. "Then maybe that's why God had to take him," he replied. Malpractice times two.

But in terms of incredibly inappropriate remarks, the one that takes the cake came after our second son, Christopher, was also stricken. A certain sanctimonious fellow left a note with my father (also a minister) saying that God had brought all this affliction on my father's tent because he had failed to exclusively use the King James Version of the Bible in his preaching.

The problem is, when you're simply struggling to survive, and wondering *just as much as everybody else* why such a catastrophe has befallen you, you're tempted to believe nonsense like this, because anything, even a lie, seems to provide a more secure footing than the instability of not knowing.

Speaking for myself and all the "Charlies" of this world, let me say to the judges and critics who seem to multiply when tragedy strikes: *Don't play God with us.*

Megaphonic Expertise

Since Charlie's still in the pit, let's observe how the advice-giver tries to help. Equipped with one of those fancy new electronic megaphones (indoors, he wears a wireless mike), the advisor struts around the pit (careful not to get too close lest he get his white shoes dirty) shouting instructions. "You should try my five principles for pit escapement, or my four foundations for worry-free living. Or how about three steps to overcoming adversity? Name it, claim it, pretend it doesn't hurt. If you will believe in your heart there is no pit, and confess with your mouth that you are standing on solid ground, your problems will disappear. There are no tragedies, after all, only opportunities for God to manifest his power in your life."

When Naomi was eighteen months old, spinal meningitis stole the hearing in her right ear. Three days after Christmas 1987, at forty-five years of age, she woke up to find herself totally deaf from the delayed effect of the same disease.

What hindered her recovery most was not all the lifestyle adjustments required, though these were formidable enough, but "those who insisted that by going to some healing service I would be miraculously healed—or the pastor-'friend' who wanted to pray for revelation of something in my past that was hindering my healing," Naomi wrote. "They looked on it as some temporary testing by God and said we just needed to pray the right way. At the same time I was trying to accept the permanence of it. I do believe some are healed miraculously, but I felt I was not one of them, and to keep insisting that I go to some prayer meeting so they could pray for me was hindering the grief process. They were not accepting what I was trying to accept. When someone's husband dies and is buried, you don't pray over the wife that he'll come back—that's essentially what they were doing."

When you're in the pit, a veritable plethora of advisors will arise who think themselves qualified to tell you: "Do this; don't do that; get on with living; stop feeling sorry for yourself; don't worry, be happy"—ad nauseum.

To all of them, from all of us: *Get real.*

I Am You and You Are Me and We Are All Together

The third approach, identification, occurs when a helper, seeing Charlie's predicament, feels for the poor guy so much he jumps right into the pit with him.

Based on the surveys I got back, identifiers are not as easy to critique, perhaps because sympathetic friends are better than nothing. After all, if Charlie gives a pity party and nobody comes, he feels worse than he did before. If you dive into that muck with him, Charlie will feel better for a while, but you'll both eventually drown.

Identification is one reason bars are so full; there may not be any answers beyond the anesthesia of alcohol, but at least misery has company, an essential commodity for people who have no intention of getting out of their pit because muck-treading is less threatening than having to face the unknowns of the cold, cruel world. If you're going to become an effective helper you'll have to learn the difference between sympathy and empathy, or you'll keep getting drawn into the pit without realizing why.

If my own personal experience tells anything, sometimes people become helpers (even professional helpers) partly because of their own needs to settle unresolved issues.

When this is true, they gravitate toward clients with problems similar to their own. And if they're not careful, they end up jumping into pits with a lot of people. If they're Olympic-level helpers, they may tread muck superbly with "Charlie," maybe even set a world record, but if another helper doesn't come along and rescue them both, Charlie and this would-be helper will eventually go under.

Some people are driven into the healing professions by a need to be needed. Certainly, if these factors can affect trained professionals, you need to be aware of them, too. I want to be clear, though. I'm not denigrating caring. A little caring goes an awfully long way in helping a heartbroken friend. But here are a few questions to ask yourself:

- Do I feel driven to solve Charlie's problem for him?
- Do I feel so involved I'm being absorbed by him?
- When Charlie talks, am I mad at the things he's mad at, offended by (or even bitter at) the sources of his heartbreak?
- When he blames anyone or anything for making him unhappy, do I find myself in full support?
- Do the things he shares remind me of my own woes, which I then freely share with him?
- How do you feel when Charlie expresses his own doubts and fears, especially when they relate to faith and even

border on blasphemy? If you're afraid, it may be that he is verbalizing the way *you feel*, but have never dared to state.

- If your heartbroken friend is a different gender than you, do you struggle with sexual desires or fantasies when you talk together about heartbreak? If so, this may be because you need to give or receive comfort in this ultimate sense. But this solution will certainly not help your friend, because the need lies *within you*. (WARNING: Get out before you both get burned!)

You Are You, and I Am Me . . . But I Do Care

If you want to help Charlie, go get a ladder, put it into his pit, climb down and say, "Hey, friend, you're not alone. I want you to know I care, and that's why I've come. I'll stay as long as it takes, but when you're ready to climb out of this muck, we'll do it together."

The main difference between sympathy and empathy is not necessarily the intensity of emotional involvement with your heartbroken friend. Your feelings may be *more intense* in empathy, for instance, when Charlie decides he's not ready to get out, even though you can see the hurt is killing him. But that's *his problem*. Yours is to find a way to love him back to life, in Jesus' name. Your reason for trying to help him is because he needs it, not because you have something to prove, or some hole to fill in your own psyche.

It's a matter of goals, really. What is the goal of your involvement with your heartbroken friend? If you are wholeheartedly committed to helping him find his way beyond heartbreak, regardless of the personal cost to you, you have a servant-heart. This is the key element in empathetic comforting, and the integrating core of loving. Although the word *servant* never occurs in the "Love Chapter," it is used elsewhere to describe what motivated Jesus to enter our heartbroken world to heal our hurts on their own terms (and turf):

> Each of you should look not only to your own interests, but also to the interests of others. Your attitude should be the same as that of Christ Jesus:
>
> Who, being in very nature God, did not consider equality with God something to be grasped, but made himself nothing, taking the very nature of a servant, being made in human likeness.
>
> And being found in appearance as a man, he humbled himself and became obedient to death—even death on a cross!
>
> (Phil. 2:4-8)

This was empathic love, fulfilling his own words: "Greater love has no one than this, that one lay down his life for his friends" (John 15:13). This empathic sacrificial love had a goal: "Let us fix our eyes on Jesus, the author and perfecter of our faith, who for the joy set before him endured the cross, scorning its shame" (Heb. 12:2). His "joy" was his vision of our salvation, another word for which is *wholeness*.

When this is your only goal for your heartbroken friend, and your motive is that of a servant-friend, you have embraced the way of therapeutic loving, with its pain as well as its joys, the only approach that can truly help your heartbroken friend.

Examples of Servant-Friendship

It's rare, but some people seem to have a special gift for helping in creative and practical ways:

- Sandra, the woman with multiple sclerosis, said: "A friend brought flowers from her garden, so I could see what was blooming. I missed all of spring, except for those flowers. People sent cards, which had never meant much to me before, but suddenly conveyed caring. My husband came and fed me soup, something so unlike him. People came with food and helped clean the house. A neighbor and her husband figured out a way to wash my hair while I was on a stretcher—and came every week for months, 'til I could use the shower."

- Rachel, whose two-and-a-half-year-old son drowned in their pool, described an immobilizing grief, during which her sister even helped bathe her. Later on, she said, "I had one Christian friend who took time to do a weekly Bible study with me, as I desired more privacy and had such personal needs. She prayed with me and for me for a year and I love her for her commitment."

- Christa, whose severely handicapped daughter lived four years, said she appreciated, "... people who dared to invade our defenses to play with our kids, wash our dishes, people who dared to love Ruth as Ruth, who talked and played with her, who looked beyond her lacking abilities to interact with the beautiful child within."

- Diana, after struggling with infertility, became pregnant, but miscarried. The same week she injured her back and spent seven weeks in bed, in pain and unable to function.

Thirteen months later, she miscarried again. "A friend wrote down the numbers of Psalms that especially spoke to the brokenhearted and gave the list to me, explaining they'd helped her," Diana said. "A friend asked me how I was feeling and then listened without telling me how I 'ought' to feel. She also did special things on days that had special significance to my pain—for example, a bag of cookies on the Sunday I returned to church. Sundays were especially painful, both due to the perennial presence of women whose babies were alive and growing, and the awareness of my brokenness before God."

- Jenny, with whose story we began this chapter, had a casual friend who sent her two to three cards a month that said, "I know you hurt, and I care." Another friend would come and take her shopping or to lunch. But the greatest love she experienced was from her husband.

"Our counselor knelt in front of us," she said, "emphasizing that we were different and we would grieve differently and we needed to respect each other's way through this and support each other wherever we were. Our marriage, good before, is stronger now."

For Reflection or Discussion

1. After Jenny's daughter died of a self-inflicted gunshot wound, Jenny needed somebody with "love enough to carry a piece of my pain." If anyone has ever done this for you, share whatever you feel comfortable revealing about that experience.

If several people describe what friends did for them, make a list of common themes.

How is this the meaning of: "Carry each other's burdens, and in this way you will fulfill the law of Christ" (Gal. 6:2)? If we are under grace, what can the "law of Christ" be?

2. Contrast Jenny's non-Christian friends, who were "there" for her, with the responses of her pastor, her Christian friend who leveled with her, and her own brother.

   Rate their relative effectiveness in "carrying a piece of the pain." Can you think of reasons why each "comforter" was more or less helpful?

   Role-play a conversation where all five parties are trying to help Jenny at the same time.

   Debrief afterward, first with the "role players," and then including the observers.

   Discuss the differences between the identifier and the soul mate, along with the dangers of the former style, both to the comforter and to the one he is trying to help.

3. Review the "questions to ask yourself" and how each of them can keep you from falling into your friend's pit. Are there other issues to avoid, also?

4. If you sense this dynamic is taking place between another person and someone she is trying to help, how might you intervene?

5. How can empathic helping increase a helper's own pain? When this happens, what can be done about it?

6. Why are goals so crucial if we really want to help a particular friend? List some examples of goals, and discuss

both the positives and negatives of each in terms of yourself and the person you wish to help.

7. As our servant, Jesus entered the heartbreak of human existence like no one before or since. List characteristics of his servant-love, citing any Scriptures that come to mind, including those mentioned in the text.

    After creating this list, see if you can identify a pattern that someone who really wants to become a better helper could emulate.

    Finally, on a personal level, choose a short-term goal in this process of change, and write out a prayer that expresses both your goals and your commitment to growth. If group members wish to share these goals with each other, end by praying that they would become a reality.

Chapter 6

Life goes on

But sometimes your friend will need an invitation.

Brenda was in the kitchen when she heard the sound of the glass breaking. She ran to the family room, and there was Celeste, her six-year-old, facing away from her, saying, "Momma, I think I'm cut."

Brenda's little girl had run, full tilt, into the sliding glass door, not realizing it was shut, and one of the pieces had sliced the left side of Celeste's face from her mouth back to her ear and then down her neck, barely missing her jugular vein.

"Half her face was lying down on her chest," Brenda said. "I ran over and pulled it back up in place and held it and started walking slowly backwards, talking to her, and yelling for somebody to dial the doctor.

"We called for an ambulance, but while we waited, there I was, holding Celeste, with her looking at me with these huge eyes saying, 'Momma, am I okay?'"

Finally the ambulance arrived. Celeste had lost a lot of blood, but since her vital signs were stable, the ambulance crew didn't do much except take off for the hospital, twenty miles away, at eighty miles per hour down Ute Pass in the snow.

For Celeste, the crisis was over; several hundred stitches took care of that. For Brenda, however, it had just begun. She described a sensation common to several of our group's participants, "There was a rattle that went through my entire body—I'll never forget *the sound of my heart breaking*, before the ambulance even got there. I don't know how else to describe it.

"In the hospital there was a cleaning lady who asked what had happened," she continued. "I told her Celeste had had an accident. The bandage had just been taken off that morning, and there were hundreds of sutures. That cleaning lady looked at her and said, 'Oh, didn't that ruin her!'"

Fighting for Equilibrium

The next time Brenda heard that sentiment expressed, it was from *one of her own relatives*, who said, "Maybe you're still in shock because it ruined her appearance."

Naturally, any caring mother would be worried how to help her recently disfigured daughter cope. While Brenda's relative wanted to straighten out Brenda's attitude, Brenda was worrying what she was going to say the first time the school kids called Celeste "scarface."

"When that day came," Brenda said, "all I could do was sit and rock her and cry with her. As a parent you're supposed to be able to help your kids and give them reasons and help make everything okay. But I found out sometimes that's not possible.

"The best I could do was tell Celeste that we all have scars in our lives—imperfections and flaws—and it just happens that yours will be visible all your life. We'll have to handle it together."

But the more Brenda identified with Celeste's needs, the more she distanced herself from her family and friends. This is one of the most devastating effects of a significant loss—a profound sense of separation, even dissociation, from those who should be closest to us . . . sometimes from life itself.

"It threw me for a loop for a long, long time," she admitted. "I couldn't pray; I couldn't sing. I went to church, but I didn't know why I was there or if I really cared anymore. My husband at that time [she's since remarried—another common result of devastating loss] was an introverted person. We had very poor communication, which I'm sure I didn't help overcome. But he wasn't there at the time of the accident, and he didn't hold her face up and have the blood running all over his hands," she said. "I don't think he ever understood my feelings."

Beyond that, the very small, traditional church Brenda was attending believed that if you belong to the Lord, everything's fine: You're covered, life's wonderful, Jesus is good, and so forth. So when the accident happened they seemed to reflect, *Well, somebody's being punished.*

But Brenda could never understand why a six-year-old child should have to go through the rest of her life with this kind of problem. So she withdrew to the only refuge she trusted—inside herself. She tried to be the strong mother with the right answers, but she didn't have anybody to talk to. Partly because of this isolation, Brenda slowly slid into mental illness.

"I'm sure the church group prayed for us," she said. "But nobody knew how to help me. I was locked inside myself, so ill for a long time. I begged my husband to put me in a mental institution. I contemplated suicide several times and came very close to trying it once. The mind does strange things."

Fringe People Need Somebody

Thankfully, accidents like this are relatively rare. On the other hand, Brenda—a regular Christian person I worked with—was so surprised by this catastrophe that she got "beamed" into a very personal twilight zone, without warning, and without any way to defend herself.

The reason I've included her story is not because it's so different, however, but because it's so *similar* to the way many believers desperately try to process heartbreak—which usually sneaks up on you, as it did with Brenda, grabs you by the throat and refuses to let go.

Initially, heartbroken people simply try to cope, to survive, to somehow get beyond the crisis, as Brenda did when she pressed her daughter's face back in place as if by some superhuman effort she could glue the flesh where it should be and everything would return to normal.

> Brenda—a regular Christian person I worked with—was so surprised by this catastrophe that she got "beamed" into a very personal twilight zone, without warning, and without any way to defend herself.

For this mother, as for most survivors, normal never returns—it can't, too many factors have changed —and the main issue becomes to what degree, if at all, they will be able to adjust to the "new normal."

During this adjustment process, which can seem to take forever, "comforters" often begin in the wrong place in their attempt to help. They start with *spiritual issues*, as if some prayer or spiritual change of heart could cure a problem like the one Brenda faced. This heartbroken mother's real problem was that she desperately needed somebody to meet her where she was and invite her back into life again. But there wasn't anybody. There almost never is.

You see, Brenda wasn't just depressed, and she wasn't being selfish, as if Celeste's beauty or lack of it somehow built up or diminished her mother's ego. Yes, she was besieged with guilt for not having protected her daughter from such a calamity. But nobody in Brenda's rather typical relational circle got her point: *Something has happened here of monumental importance—to Celeste, and to me. Our dreams have died and what I need, what I long for most, is a friend to say, "It's okay, Brenda. If I were you, I'd feel the same way. I'd have similar questions, especially in relation to God."*

What Brenda actually received was silence, distance, exile—all of which, in her psychological state, she could only interpret as judgment: "Too bad. So sad. You're bad."

Into the Wilderness

Here was a brokenhearted woman, trying to find her way through an emotional, relational, and spiritual wasteland. A map and a compass might have been helpful, and perhaps that's what her church friends thought they were giving her through their exhortations. But the wilderness can be an intensely frightening experience if you've never been there before, or you've never even heard that such a place exists.

In some ways, Brenda was like the lost sheep in Jesus' parable of the shepherd who leaves the ninety-nine to fend for themselves in order to search for the lost one until he finds it. When the lost one is found, the shepherd puts it on his shoulders, carries it home, and then invites his friends and neighbors to a celebration.

A shepherd who really loves *all* his sheep will consistently put the recovery of one lost sheep ahead of the maintenance of the rest, and *rejoice more* over the recovery of that *single individual* than over the fact that the rest of the flock never strayed.

In relation to the lostness that comes with a broken heart, this has significant implications for the way pastors view their responsibilities. If my perceptions are correct, most of us focus most of our energies on the larger group, for a variety of reasons including *their demand, or at least their expectation*, that we will do so. When pastoral "success" is measured by growth—primarily numerical and financial—and the preacher is expected to spend thirty hours in preparation and another fifteen in visiting the "faithful," not to mention various other duties, those lost sheep are on their own. The message sent is, "Find your own way back to the fold."

If the pastor does spend an "inordinate amount of time" away from the flock, seeking the lost sheep, he may be castigated or worse for investing his energies in people who have little potential to contribute and who may, instead, divert resources because of their many needs.

Like the Pharisees whose indictment Jesus was answering with this parable, the consensus of the flock still may be: "She disconnected herself, let her find her own way back. *We* haven't moved, and we'll still be here when she sees the error of her ways and decides to return."

Jesus' response was *to go looking* for the lost ones and then carry them "home" on his shoulders and celebrate. Whether it was the outcasts, the hurting, the disenfranchised, disabled, or broken, he treated them all with this kind of loving acceptance and respect. This was God's grace breaking into human experience, yet it irritated those who thought Jesus ought to pay a lot more attention to good people like them.

If you really want to help disconnected people, you may have to contend with attitudes like these, at the same time you'll have to risk sharing their disorientation, anxiety, and sorrow—coming face-to-face with your own relative lostness even as you walk together, or you carry one of them, out of the wilderness. You don't have to be an ordained minister in order to do this, but you do need to fulfill the root meaning of the word *pastor*, which is "shepherd."

Role Plays and Reality

Sometimes pastors need pastors in this very same way. For a long time after Jonathan's death, I wandered in my own wilderness—lost, disconnected, isolated, wounded, and broken. More than any other time in my life, I was personally, relationally, and professionally at risk as I wallowed in the "Slough of Despond," unable and sometimes unwilling to do much of anything else.

During one of our group meetings, Dan and Mary (the pastor and wife whose daughter was killed) role-played a visit to the parsonage late on a Saturday morning about six months after Jonathan's death, to see if they could somehow help me get reconnected with life. My wife is grocery shopping with a couple of young mothers from the church, in the nearest town —thirty miles away. I am still in my robe, unshowered and unshaven when the doorbell rings. I am familiar with their experience of losing a daughter, so I let my guard down. Here's an adapted version of how it went:

> Dave: Dan and Mary, what a surprise.
>
> Dan: Did we come at a bad time?
>
> Dave: Yes.
>
> Dan: Good to see you. Just finishing breakfast?
>
> Dave: I'm just kind of lounging around here.
>
> Dan: How are things going for you these days?
>
> Dave: Hah!
>
> Dan: Still pretty tough?
>
> Dave: Yup. The hard part is having to get up and preach every week, and teach Sunday school and do the Wednesday night service. I just barely make it through sometimes.
>
> Dan: I'm sure your people don't realize the load you're carrying right now.
>
> Dave: They want me to carry on like nothing happened.
>
> Mary: That's impossible; you can't do it.
>
> Dan: It's been six months now. How long do you think it will take before you'll be able to function again?
>
> Dave: I don't even know if I *want* to function again, or even what that would mean. Seems like I only leave the house to go to church and preach.
>
> Dan: Not even to play golf? One reason I came by today is because I need a good golf partner next Saturday to play with

me and a couple other guys.

Dave: (Sighs) I don't know, Dan. It's just a lot easier to stay home. I don't think I could stand being out. It's such a small town, and they're probably talking about me. It's just easier to stay home.

Dan: If they're talking about you, it's because they wish they could help in some way. They just don't know how.

Dave: I don't either. I thought I did, but it was just words before. Now I don't know how to help . . . what I believe. Seems like I'm a robot, just going through the motions.

Dan: I know what that's like, but sometimes we have to get hold of ourselves and realize we have a life to live.

Dave: Did you ever feel like dying instead?

Dan: Yes.

Dave: I'd rather die, instead.

Mary: I questioned everything I had ever believed, everything. But I discovered one little piece at a time will put it back together. It takes time, and it's a very personal journey. I'm sure it's different for you and your wife. You're probably not in the same places, but that's okay, too.

Dan: I remember when we had suffered with this, wallowing in our grief for so long. One night I told Mary, "We've got to pick up our lives and go on; start to be happy and smile again." It took a conscious effort to decide we were going to get over it, going to make it. Maybe you're getting close to that place in your life.

Dave: I don't know, man. It sure doesn't feel that way. It feels like I'm going in the other direction.

Dan: We make an effort to recover, and healing comes with

our efforts. Are you sure you won't play golf with me next Saturday? You could help me keep my ball on the course.

Dave: I'm sorry, Dan. I just can't do it. Maybe another time.

Dan: I'll call you Thursday to see if you've changed your mind.

Dave: Ok. Call Thursday, but really . . . you should try to find another partner.

Different Folks, Different Strokes

I had a good friend named Ed, a fellow pastor who did help me, though it took me years to understand how much. Ed came looking for me, just making himself available, without implying that I needed fixing and he was going to do it for me.

"You need to get away?" he would say. "I know where there's a cabin you could use."

"You like fishing?" he asked, even though he knew I did. "There's some pretty good places up here." And he took me to one of them, a canal above a dam, where walleyes—big ones—fed after dark. The only reason I knew this for sure was that while Ed and I had been casting for what seemed like hours, an older fellow drove up, climbed onto the walkway over the dam, and started reeling in monsters one after the other. He even gave us lures like his to use, but for some reason he had the magic touch and we didn't. Before he left, he gave us one of his fish, which we took back to the cabin and cooked in bacon fat over a pot-bellied stove. What a great meal that was!

We really didn't get together enough, but Ed was a shepherd looking for a lost sheep. I don't remember a lot of what he said, but I do remember that *Ed let me be me*. He asked a lot of questions, but I knew it was not to pry, but because he really wanted to understand what the wilderness was like. And I don't think he ever judged me if (or when) my answers were less than orthodox.

Every heartbroken person needs a friend like that. If you're going to connect with a person who's out on that periphery, you'll need a double portion of acceptance, gentleness, understanding, and kindness or your beneficent intrusion may feel like pity, condescension, or criticism to the person you're trying to reach.

Here are some suggestions for how to do this:

- Validate your friend's sense of disconnection. Just being accepted by somebody may help her open up even more to you.

- Be gently persistent. Your friend may not be ready this week to go to a baseball game (or golfing), so don't force anything. But keep offering. Someday he'll take you up on it.

- Search for some activity to share, even if it means attending something—from opera to demolition derby—that you wouldn't personally choose.

- If your friend's loss was traumatic and sudden, every week for at least six months, stop in and let her know you're thinking of her. During these visits, try to discern where she's at, and tailor your next offer of something to do to match her status.

- If you have small children, and you want to help an older widow, when the time seems right invite her to become a surrogate grandma. One physician-friend with five kids recently asked one of his patients if she would like to go to the zoo with his family. The woman replied, "Oh, thank you. I'd really love that. I've been feeling really lonely lately."

- Regardless of what your friend says about God or anything else, steadfastly refuse to reject her. Eventually, she'll realize you really have journeyed into the wasteland of her pain, and she'll be much more open to walking with you out of it.

- Investigate what support groups are meeting in your area, then invite your friend *to go with you* to the one that seems to best address her need. Attend all the sessions with her, and use what's said there as a basis for your continuing dialogue.

For Reflection or Discussion

1. Suppose you were visiting in the hospital with your friend Brenda when the cleaning woman commented on Celeste's awful scars: "Oh, didn't that ruin her!" What would you have said or done?
   Has anything like that ever been said to you? If so, describe how it felt and how you responded.

2. You're visiting Brenda in her home when Celeste comes crying in the door from school saying, "Momma, they called me 'scarface'!" Answer the same questions as above.

3. Brenda said she could "hear" her own heart break. What do you think she was describing? If something like that has happened to you, try to describe it in different terms.

4. What were the causes of Brenda's mental illness? If she were your friend, how would you try to help her?

5. When they try to help, why do "comforters" often begin with their heartbroken friend's *spiritual* issues:
    - ❑ Because that's the key to everything else.
    - ❑ Because the Bible only addresses those issues.
    - ❑ Because this may, in fact, be God's judgment or discipline, and, if so, somebody needs to point it out.
    - ❑ Because feeling with (or just being with) somebody is much harder than exhorting him to get right with God.
    - ❑ Other:

6. The children of Israel spent forty years wandering in the wilderness, but God used that time to work in their lives. What are some of the parallel values of a personal "wilderness experience"?
    - ❑ to refine faith
    - ❑ to teach dependence
    - ❑ to clarify identity
    - ❑ to extinguish a victim mentality
    - ❑ all of the above
    - ❑ Other:

7. Do you think there are pressures on your pastor that keep him (or her) from seeking and restoring the lost sheep of your congregation? If so, identify them. After making a list, brainstorm what you as a group might do to help change this.

8. Have you ever felt like a lost sheep? If so, describe the experience and what was most helpful in finding your way home.

9. In Jesus' day, the lepers were outcasts, yet he healed them, even touched them. Read Matthew 8:1-4 and discuss how this passage affects your view of Christ's "making God visible" to those who are treated like outcasts by society today. Are some treated similarly by the church? If so, what could you do to "make God visible" to them?

10. What images or thought pictures come to mind when you think of Jesus as the good shepherd.

11. The story of David's treatment of Mephibosheth is one of the most touching pictures of kindness in the Scriptures. Read 2 Samuel 4:4; 9:1-13, and list the ways the new king treated his potential rival as his own *kindred*.

    Identify elements of David's attitudes and actions that can be universalized to any situation where a heartbroken friend needs godly kindness.

    Once you have completed this list, review it, looking for parallels to the way that God has demonstrated his kindness toward you. How might living with a more continual awareness of this expression of God's grace become a powerful motivator and model for you as you seek to nudge your marginalized friend back toward life again?

Chapter 7

What to do when you don't know what to do

Quite often what your friend needs most is not a card or a sermon. . . .

Arlene looked out the window anxiously as the thunder from the approaching storm kept getting louder. *This one's going right over us,* she thought. *Where's Bobby?*

Her seven-year-old had been playing in the yard across the street. Arlene relaxed just a little when she noticed the kids, huddled under the trees, preparing to bravely wait out the storm as if it were just another adventure to add to their seemingly endless escapades together.

Suddenly, out of nowhere, a reddish fireball appeared in the sky, struck one of the trees, followed its trunk to the ground and disappeared with a frightening roar. For Arlene, even more alarming was a reality that took a split second to register: *Bobby? Bobby was under that tree! No!*

Arlene rushed outside, barefoot, through the mud to the adjoining yard, to find Bobby lying dead in the soft evergreen needles, his eyebrows and eyelashes burned off. She tried mouth-to-mouth resuscitation, but got no response. She didn't know how to do CPR—nobody did in those days.

There was no rescue squad, either. So Arlene sat there in shock, holding Bobby and waiting for a doctor to come, trying to convince herself, *This isn't happening. It's not real!* But every time she looked at Bobby, a different reality iced her soul.

The doctor's words confirmed what her heart rejected but her mind knew as truth. "I'm sorry," he said. "He's gone. There's nothing we can do. You should go home. I'll wait here with him and take care of everything."

Sadly, Arlene finally consented, slowly dragging herself back to her own house, wishing her husband wasn't out of town. *Have to call him. How can I tell him? How can I tell anybody? Who should I call?* She pondered these and many other unwelcome questions as she slumped heartbroken in a chair, alone.

Within an hour, however, "A neighbor lady whom I barely knew came in the house," she remembers, "and not knowing what to do or say . . . she washed my feet."

Profound Simplicities

Although it's been decades since Bobby died, Arlene's most enduring positive memory from that whole horrifying experience is a simple gesture by someone who was neither a believer nor a close friend. Caring, when it connects with brokenness this directly, is more substantial than a hundred funeral sermons or a thousand cards of consolation.

Of course, we're dealing with selective recall here, and you might want to dismiss such a simple act as insignificant compared to other things that must have been said or done by pastors, Christian friends, or others who tried to help. But if Arlene's memory is anything like mine, one function of time in relation to these issues is that it sorts out what was valuable and important from what wasn't.

> *Caring, when it connects with brokenness this directly, is more substantial than a hundred funeral sermons or a thousand cards of consolation.*

We pastors, especially, think our most important ministry in situations like this is functionary—visitation, counseling, preparation, and presentation of a sermon, advising or helping with or even totally handling the funeral arrangements.

But if the heartbroken people we've tried to help would level with us, we'd be both surprised and chagrined to discover what really mattered *to them*, which is, quite often, the way someone met a physical need.

For instance, Gerry, who pastors in a small town, is fondly remembered not so much for his many "ministerial" functions but because when there's a death in the community (not just among his parishioners) he goes out, buys a ham, and takes it to the family's home. "This is for you to use wherever you need it," he says. If they invite him in, fine. If they don't he leaves the gift and goes home. Either way, he's become part of that family's permanent mental home movie of the events surrounding their loss.

Obviously, you don't have to be a pastor to do something like this. In fact, in our group's discussion of this aspect of heartmending (and in the surveys returned to me) the people who most helped were usually laypersons. Here are a few examples:

- Martha's neighbor would often slip in the back door, take the dirty laundry home and then bring it back later, clean and neatly folded. Immediately after Martha's husband died, this friend gathered up all the husband's soiled clothes, took them to her home, washed them, and packed them in a box. About a month later she said to Martha, "I have Bruce's things. What do you want to do with them?"

  Sometimes this woman did Martha's dishes or cleaned the house. Often she would leave several plates of food on the counter because she knew Martha was struggling with even simple things like feeding her two young children.

  Beyond the many practical ways that Martha's "angel" of kindness helped, perhaps the most significant long-term component of her caring was that *it expressed love, with no strings attached.*

- Jennifer needed help during the final stages of her husband's bout with lung cancer. "Men from the church came to visit David, and do household chores he couldn't do. Within the first month after David's death, some men finished projects he had started, took the trash to the dump and mowed the yard."

- Mary and Kim were friends before Mary's daughter died, but shortly after this event, Kim, a grandmother with a business to run, arrived at Mary's doorstep one morning, armed with deli food and a willing spirit. "We were writing thank-you notes," Mary recalls, "and Kim came in and said, 'What can I do?' She offered to help us write, but we felt we had to do it in our own language. So after a while, she said, 'Come on, Mary. Let's get this house cleaned up.'"

Coming from anybody else, that offer might have offended Mary, but coming from Kim, it didn't. "She took the time, she gave us her day, the whole day," Mary said. "She brought lunch and ate with us. And she got me in gear as we threw some stuff in the washer. The house wasn't that despicable. She was saying, 'Come on, life goes on. Let's function.'"

Kim cared enough to drive a long distance to personally try to help Mary and Dan cope with their loss. A phone call, card, or flowers might have expressed her concern, but in person she could really see and address what needed the most attention.

Being There Is Just the Beginning

If this book has had any common theme thus far, it's that *being there* when your heartbroken friend needs someone to share the pain is the most important factor in being a mender of hearts.

But if you're willing to pay the cost, being there is just part of becoming involved in some practical and personal way in addressing the unique needs inherent in every person's wilderness experience.

When the people of Israel wandered in their wilderness, waiting for the unbelieving generation to die, the Lord provided manna to eat and water to drink. Their clothing did not rot, nor did their feet swell as they traveled many, many miles in fulfilling God's program for refining their faith.

There are many lessons in this biblical example, but one that applies here is that even if your friend's desert journey is a direct judgment for a specific sin (highly unlikely, but possible), God himself will not abandon him or her, but will continue to provide for even their most basic needs. How can we dare do less?

Most often, God's provision is expressed through people. In the Old Testament, the prophet Elijah was sent to the widow at Zarephath, to meet her needs as well as his own. It was the middle of a drought through which God was judging King Ahab, and the brook by which Elijah had been staying had dried up. When the prophet met the woman, she was gathering sticks to make a fire on which she planned to prepare the last meal for herself and her son. But because she was faithful enough to first make from her meager supply of flour and olive oil a meal for Elijah, the Lord never let her jar of flour or jug of oil run dry until the rains came again, and both her needs and Elijah's were met during that entire time. In effect, God provided for each of them through the other (see 1 Kings 17:1-16).

Elijah's successor Elisha was also God's instrument to meet the physical needs of another widow who was in desperate straits. Her husband, one of the "company of the prophets," had died, and now their creditor was coming to take the woman's two sons as his slaves.

All this heartbroken woman had left in her house was a little bit of oil. Elisha told her to borrow empty jars from all her neighbors. "Don't ask for just a few," he instructed her. "Then go inside and shut the door behind you and your sons. Pour oil into all the jars."

After all the jars were filled, the miraculous flow of oil stopped. The widow sold the oil, paid her debts, and still had enough left over for her and her sons to live on. The point: God is concerned with more than "spiritual" needs. He takes a personal interest in our physical needs, many of which he meets through other people (see 2 Kings 4:1-7).

In the New Testament, Jesus often addressed physical needs. His very first miracle, when he turned water to wine so the wedding celebration at Cana could continue, is testimony enough that the Lord's interests went far beyond merely saving souls. He fed the 5,000 because they were hungry. He healed untold numbers—the blind, the lame, the deaf, the lepers, and many others—because *they were better off well*. Of course, in each case, there was a spiritual lesson. But from the perspective of those healed, the main lesson was that Jesus cared enough to apply his miraculous power at the point of their overwhelming need.

The strongest indictment of the early church's neglect of people in need was made by James, the half-brother of Jesus, perhaps because he had seen the Lord in action. "What good is it, my brothers," he asks, "if a man claims to have faith but has no deeds? Can such faith save him? Suppose a brother or sister is without clothes and daily food. If one of you says to him, 'Go, I wish you well; keep warm and well fed,' but does nothing about his physical needs, what good is it?" (James 2:14-16).

In one confrontation with the teachers of his day (see Mark 7:9-13), Jesus pointed out the hypocrisy of religion that lacked a heart for people's real needs, even the needs of one's own father and mother. Even though the Law commanded, "Honor your father and mother," the religious tradition nullified this if what might have been available to help them had been promised to God, instead.

The result was that because of a man's vows, his religious teachers *would not allow him to help his parents*. The conflict here is not just between interpretations of the Law. The basic issue is the separation of physical and spiritual realities, or the secular and the sacred. In Jesus' view, even when a man had promised his present (and future) excess financial resources to God—a commendable spiritual act in itself—meeting the needs of his aging parents still took precedence.

James was concerned that the church might slide backward toward the attitude that spiritual issues are all that matter. Sometimes this perspective still drives people when it comes to helping the heartbroken among us. Thankfully, however, some heart-menders understand the crucial importance of addressing more practical needs, too.

Help When I Needed It Most

Several bereaved parents described practical help that had a long-term impact:

- Sharlene's two-year-old son Jesse died after struggling with cancer. During this ordeal, Sharlene's church friends were a real godsend. "My friends and church family were a continual support," she wrote. "There was nothing anyone could *say* that made me feel better. However, what people *did* helped more than anything. When I was unable to function properly someone would bring a meal, clean, or help with my other child. Keeping my home in a functioning order was so important to me, but I was unable to do it.

    "My heart breaks for people who don't have a pastor or church like we have," she said. "Our pastor was our friend—he was constantly there for us. We also had 'deacon care groups.' Our deacon and his wife made many trips to the hospital with us. He even went so far as to pack his office work into a briefcase and take us to Philadelphia for Jesse's tests. He waited and did his work all day and was there for us when we needed him most.

"In our church we also have a lady who plans meals for anyone coming home from the hospital. We always had a meal waiting when we came home from a long day of chemotherapy."

- Andrea was driving the car when it slid off an icy road and into a telephone pole, killing her six-year-old, Jamie. "One close friend became our 'chauffeur' and drove us to the funeral home, the florist, etc., that whole week when we were unable to think straight," Andrea wrote.

  "Someone else organized meals to be brought to us for several weeks. At the reviewal, our 'chauffeur' and his wife brought us water and encouraged us to take breaks when things got too emotionally draining. Others helped by staying at our home during the reviewal and funeral, in case of a break-in."

  Writing only four months after the tragedy, Andrea added, "A few very faithful friends have continued to express concern and love by listening (most important) and by calling us instead of waiting for us to call them. It was Jamie's birthday this time—three people sent plants or flowers, and many remembered by sending a 'Thinking of you' card. Ashley, our four-year-old daughter, has received a letter or package every week for these past four months from her aunt and cousin, and they have tried in many ways to establish a real closeness and bond with her, for siblings seem to get lost in the shuffle."

- Wendy had two miscarriages in a row after trying for years to conceive, but some people, including family members didn't seem to want to acknowledge her sense of loss as legitimate.

"It was only with the people who made the effort to come to our home that we truly let go and sought comfort," she wrote. "Over the phone, we tried much harder to be brave and put up a good front. With a real, live person in front of us, we were a lot more able to receive comfort. It's almost as if the family members who couldn't get in the car and drive thirty minutes were silently saying the event wasn't all that catastrophic."

Based on her experience, to comfort someone facing a similar loss, Wendy would "be on their doorstep in a flash, with something highly caloric. I'd make a date once a week or so for the first month just to see how they're doing," she wrote. "I'd also make a note of when the event occurred (if practical) and let them know on that date that I realize how hard the anniversary must be."

Laying Up Treasures in Heaven

Sometimes the heartbroken friend we're trying to help may be dying. In this case, it's not so much a question of recovery as something else—coping, preparation, or even simply saying good-bye.

- Brenda's cousin, Francine, had been diagnosed with leukemia. Just before Francine was to begin chemotherapy, she asked Brenda, "Would you go to the nurses' station, get a pair of scissors and cut my hair? I'd rather have you cut my hair real short so I'll look nice for a little while before the chemo makes it all fall out."

"I was behind her as I gave her a haircut," Brenda admitted, "and I'm sure I cried a million tears in those snips. But it's what she wanted, and if it meant that much to her to have me cut her hair instead of just having it fall out in globs, then that's what I wanted to do ... but it hurt!

"After Francine came home I asked, 'Do you want to go see the kids' ball games?' At first, she seemed afraid to say, 'Yeah,' because it was risky for her. She never knew when she might start vomiting. But she knew I was willing to take her. The only thing that mattered for me was that I wanted to make a difference for her, because there was an end coming in her life.

"So we'd go to the ball game and huddle up in a blanket, and sometimes she would say, 'I've got to go,' and she might start throwing up on the way to the truck. But we'd get home and she would say, 'I just loved that. Seeing the kids play ball just meant so much to me.'

"It was one of those rare times, when you can really give somebody a special gift," Brenda said.

- Mary's friend Linda, gorgeous and in her early forties, was dying of cancer. "She was one of the most beautiful Christians I've ever known," Mary said. "I wondered, *What can I do for Linda in these last months? How can I help her?*

"I decided that once a week I would offer to pick her up and take her for a ride. I made it clear she could say anything she wanted to. 'I want you to tell me if you're angry. When your hair falls out from the treatment, I want you to talk about it.'

"She did. She opened up, and we would just park

under a shade tree somewhere and stay as long as she wanted to, until she told me she was tired and needed to get back to bed. During those months, Linda unloaded all her feelings as we talked about whatever was on her mind.

"We even talked about her husband. 'I know Don will marry again soon, because he's just not the type that will be alone,' she said once. 'But that bothers me.' So we talked about that openly and freely. We also talked about her children, some of whom weren't Christians—a deep concern for her.

"'What are they going to do with my things, Mary?' she asked me once. It was a precious time together, and we became closer than we had been before. And toward the end, one day I said, 'Linda, I have a favor to ask of you. If you get to heaven before I do, please tell Minny I love her.'"

Of course, Linda agreed, and in the end, Mary and Linda helped each other.

Helper's Checklist to Meet Physical Needs

Perhaps the best question to ask yourself in relation to addressing physical needs is: "If Jesus were here, what would he do?" When you try to address these physical needs, you become a physical link between God's comfort and the person who needs it. You could accomplish a lot less than that. Many do. But you could never accomplish more.

Once you've resolved to become that link between God and your heartbroken friend, you may still need some suggestions for how to help. Here are a few ideas to get you started:

- hugs all around, unless this makes the huggee uncomfortable;
- clean house, but never betray your trust by telling others how dirty things are (or anything else you observe there);
- help write thank-you cards, especially the generic type that don't require a personal touch;
- financial gifts, especially if the expenses are great (start a special fund if appropriate);
- provide for child care or respite care, whichever is needed most;
- send flowers or some personalized gift if you can't be there;
- use your sphere of influence to address a unique need (for instance, to arrange a lower airline fare);
- ban from your vocabulary: "Call me if you need something";
- offer to chauffeur, especially if your friend is in shock —you could save her life, and protect others, too;
- envision or discern what needs doing by asking, "What would I need to have done for me in this situation?" Then be sure it gets done;
- offer legal or financial advice if you are qualified. Handling an estate or filing an income tax form can be formidable tasks for some people;
- pastors might develop a specific checklist for newly bereaved persons, to help them identify what to expect from as many directions as possible. (But don't forget to take the ham!)

For Reflection or Discussion

1. Can caring that connects directly with brokenness (as when Arlene's muddy feet were washed by her friend) be "more substantial than a hundred funeral sermons or a thousand cards of consolation"?
    - ❏ No doubt, though I've never experienced it.
    - ❏ I wonder, since the Truth is what really sustains anybody.
    - ❏ Consolation cards can express caring.
    - ❏ What is this, Care Bear theology?
2. If every heartbroken family has a permanent mental home movie of the events surrounding a loss, how important is it for helpers to get it right the first time?
3. The practical help that Martha's friend provided was an expression of "love without strings attached." Review 1 Corinthians 13:4-7a for aspects of love that ought to come in this form and compare this "love without strings" to the earlier phrase "love without wax." Bring in other Scripture passages that illuminate this idea, and then discuss the relative difficulty of giving or receiving this kind of love.
4. Prioritize the list below in terms of *long-term relative importance* to a church family when faced with a tragic death:
    - ❏ Picking the right funeral hymns.
    - ❏ That the funeral message includes "the gospel."
    - ❏ Keeping track of—and thanking—those who send flowers.

- ❏ Making sure the deceased's attire is nicely pressed.
- ❏ Trying to remember what's happening next.
- ❏ A hug and some shared tears from a friend who cares.
- ❏ Having prepared food delivered to the home, at least once a day for a week (a month would be better), with cooks' names clearly marked on the bottom of each bowl. But don't make the one you're helping return them.
- ❏ That the pastor came by late one night just to see how they were doing, and to pray with them.
- ❏ That the sermon answered all the *"Why"* questions.
- ❏ That the pastor, organist, and soloist all got paid.

5. One word for the Holy Spirit is *paraklete*—one called alongside (to help). In what ways might the Spirit's helping be expressed physically, as compared to the way we usually think of it? How is this an opportunity to "make God visible"?

6. Writing from prison, the apostle Paul asked his young friend Timothy for help. Read 2 Timothy 4:9-22, listing the various types of needs being expressed. Compose a modem version of this passage, beginning with the phrase, "These past few years have been heartbreaking in some ways, but. . . ."

7. Read Mark 7:6-13, and then have volunteers role-play a conversation involving a man, his aging parents who need his assistance, and the pastor of the church to which the man has pledged all his excess resources toward the multimillion dollar building program. In the middle of the ar-

gument, if there is one, have someone representing Jesus' point of view come in and arbitrate.

8. At the end of this chapter, pastors are encouraged to develop a checklist for newly bereaved persons to help them anticipate many of the things they will face. As a group, create the kind of checklist you would find most helpful in this situation. When you have identified the basic issues to be addressed, ask your pastor if he (or she) would like to have a copy.

Chapter 8

Somebody to hold me

Sometimes the best answers can't be put into words.

Rocky was a long distance runner. Many times a year his long legs propelled his slender six-foot, nine-inch frame up the grueling twelve-mile-long Pikes Peak highway and back down in less than four hours. A construction worker acquainted with hard labor, Rocky had his life changed in an instant when he leaned over to pick up something and a disc ruptured, injuring his spinal cord. Suddenly, Rocky was paralyzed below the waist, and his family became penniless in no time because the injury wasn't job-related.

For weeks, all Rocky could do, while his wife was out working, was lie in bed. He couldn't even use his own bathroom, so since they lived in the country, he would drag himself outside to use his backyard for a toilet, then back indoors to bed.

During this process, he not only lost touch with his legs, he lost touch with God. He felt abandoned and betrayed and very confused... except when his faithful friend, Glenn, would visit.

"When Glenn came to see me," Rocky said, "there wasn't

anything he could say. He didn't preach any sermons, or tell me how I should be feeling or what I should be thinking. Instead, he would actually climb into the bed with me, wrap his arms around me, and we would both cry. After he had been there, I felt like I had been bathed in love."

Rocky's issues were common to every heartbroken person who's ever lived, most of them starting with the word, "Why?" But his most helpful answer came not in words, ideas, insights or counsel, but in the form of a person. Somebody to hold him.

Betsy's husband was a pastor . . . before his adultery brought the loss of job, church, and friends—for Betsy, not just for David. As a result, Betsy struggled with low self-esteem and other emotional issues that often accompany heartbreak.

Betsy wrote that she had a few friends, at first, "who would hang in despite my bizarre behavior and the things I said, not demanding that I be rational, reasonable, immediately forgiving, nor angry." She also had a pastor-friend who sat with her "long enough so that one day God showed him a degree of the pain of rejection I was experiencing [and] he understood."

> "Why?" But his most helpful answer came not in words, ideas, insights or counsel, but in the form of a person. Somebody to hold him.

Despite her strong personal faith, Betsy resented almost any Scripture, because, she said, "I wanted Christ in the form of people to show me he/they cared." For a long while, Betsy became "deeply depressed as the current pain hooked back into a childhood of abuse—emotional and sexual. During this time," she recalled, "I would see only four or five people (as well as my nuclear family)."

Her magnified emotional pain fueled this depression. One pastor observed that she was hurting other people by her depressed behavior and that she should "pull herself together."

Within this brokenhearted woman was a frightened, bewildered child who needed this reassurance: *Even though life has dealt you an awful disappointment, things will be okay again.* But in order for these words of consolation to connect with Betsy's inner child, they had to be expressed in terms even a little girl could understand.

Insights, principles, even biblical truths were not very helpful when Betsy's anguish was compounded by the shame, guilt, and worthlessness gushing to the surface from her underground pool of hurtful memories. With her spiritual background, Betsy already *knew all she needed to know* in order to survive, with or without the help of her friends. What she really needed was somebody to hold her—metaphorically and even physically.

Hide or Seek

Now let's suppose for a moment you are Betsy's friend (or Rocky's) and you want to help her (or him) recover more quickly and more completely than either can manage alone. Your main question will be how much emotional energy you are willing to invest. Most Christian "comforters" appeal first to the mind—we'll talk more about that next chapter—but only a *person* can bind up another person's broken heart. Only a person can find the pathway into a friend's real need, enter it and share the pain until he or she decides it's time to move beyond it.

Be warned: You can't do this alone or you'll risk being overwhelmed when your friend's pain *taps into your own emotions or memories.* You'll need help, divine help. As Betsy said, and as Glenn demonstrated, *Christ in you* will demonstrate that he and you really do care. If you've been around the church much, you've heard this idea before. But in order to transform it from a concept to reality, let's look at just one example of how Jesus showed a heartbroken friend he cared.

The friend was Peter, whose denial and restoration is one of the most gripping narratives in the Gospels. Peter, the impetuous, impulsive disciple, had promised Jesus, "Even if I have to die with you, I will never disown you."

But after the disciple's third denial, Luke says that "the Lord turned and looked straight at Peter. Then Peter remembered the word the Lord had spoken to him. . . . And he went outside and wept bitterly" (Luke 22:61-62).

No half-hearted remorse here. The rugged fisherman had failed as miserably as he could possibly manage. His heart was as broken as it could be.

The next time we see Jesus and Peter together, we discover that Peter had gone back to fishing, and taken some of the others with him. After they had fished all night and caught nothing, the resurrected Jesus called to them from the shore, and told them to cast their net on the right side of the boat. As a result, they caught so many fish they couldn't even haul in the net. Peter, realizing it was the Lord, jumped overboard and waded ashore, a rather dramatic response. But something far more dramatic took place after breakfast.

> Jesus said to Simon Peter, Simon son of John, do you truly love [*agape*] me more than these?
> Yes, Lord, he [Peter] said, you know that I love [*phileo*] you.

Jesus said, "Feed my lambs."

Again Jesus said, "Simon son of John, do you truly love [*agape*] me?"

He answered, "Yes, Lord, you know that I love [*phileo*] you."

Jesus said, "Take care of my sheep."

The third time he said to him, "Simon son of John, do you love [*phileo*] me?"

Peter was hurt because Jesus asked him the third time, "Do you love me?" He said, "Lord, you know all things; you know that I love [*phileo*] you."

Jesus said, "Feed my sheep."

(John 21:15-17)

The basic lesson in this interchange isn't primarily analytical, semantic, or even theological. It's emotional. The resurrected Jesus is reinstating his fallen friend, giving him a new sense of mission—to shepherd the flock of God.

Since Jesus could have accomplished this in any way, at any time and in any place he wished, the setting, method, and words are very significant. He chose the *setting* where Peter was most competent—fishing—to demonstrate that the only way to succeed even in one's arena of competence is with divine guidance. The *method* matched Peter's denials, in reverse. And in his choice of *words* Jesus matched emotion for emotion, switching from his own word for love (*agape*) to Peter's (*phileo*) as if to accept the best Peter could manage at that moment. His unspoken message: "Peter, I know you don't agape me now, but I know that someday you will because I forgive you, and I believe in you. When you have recovered, you will strengthen your brothers."

Peter was hiding from his calling—because of his shame—

so *the Lord came seeking him*. That's the way it's been between God and humans since the Garden of Eden, and that's the way it will be until Jesus comes again. He simply will not let the members of his family languish in their pain without letting them know, from without or within, that he loves them.

And when he finds the one he seeks, he enters through *the open door*—in most cases—the emotions. He meets Peter on his own "turf" and terms, and addresses the broken man's felt need—guilt—as a way to approach a deeper need, the real need—reconciliation, renewal, and recommissioning.

If you're going to help your heartbroken friend, you'll never miss if you follow this method. Make contact first with the emotions, then the mind, then the will, and ultimately the spirit. Then support him or her until what's happening inside works its way out.

Shame—the Blight of Broken Hearts

There may be several reasons why my own recovery has taken so long, but a primary contributor was that I never had *somebody to hold me*. As a father I had failed. The little boy entrusted to me had died, and nothing anybody could say made any real difference . . . at least not for me.

In late August 1978, this image etched itself into the pages of my emotional self: It's the middle of the night and Jonathan, almost four, is standing on the little stool with his name on it, trying to throw up into the bathroom sink. For three days he's been nauseated—presumably a viral illness. I figure he'll get over it soon.

"Can I have a drink, Daddy?" he asks.

"Not yet, Jon. It might make you throw up again."

I didn't know any better. I told him what I'd always heard. How was I supposed to know that the next morning he would experience brain damage from dehydration and as a result of that, five weeks later he would die?

I, who would have died defending him against any and all threats to his life, became the means to his death; at least, that's the way it felt, and *how it felt was all that mattered* for months after the event that broke our dreams.

Doctors told us it wasn't our fault. Friends, family, everybody who knew about it assured us they wouldn't have handled it differently. But even if an angel from God had appeared, announcing my absolution, I wouldn't have accepted it.

Guilt, especially the rather abject variety experienced by bereaved parents, wraps its icy tentacles around broken hearts and refuses to yield to reason, religion, or anything in between.

On one level, I functioned. I had to. There were sermons to preach, classes to teach, weddings (and funerals) to perform, babies to dedicate, and people to counsel and lead to the Lord. But regardless of how good I became at using my own heartbreak to connect with other people's pain, I couldn't disconnect from my own. I could even help people gain freedom from their own guilt and shame, but I could not set myself free.

Everything I did became another opportunity to be guilty, as I pursued myself through the shadowy pathways of my own mind, constantly trying, convicting, and sentencing the villain to the only thing he deserved—torment (actually, he deserved to die, but torment was the closest I could come). If I broke the speed limit, I debated turning myself in. In relation to certain other infractions, I actually did turn myself in, paying one fine. Gradually during this time I sank into the quicksand of striving to live as "righteously" as I could, not so much to prove anything as to protect myself from further self-imposed penance. As the real (but unresolved) guilt I felt about having failed Jonathan attached itself to other things, I became an obsessive-compulsive person (obsessed with my self-mortification, and compelled to try to release the guilt somehow). I could tell you about the hand-washing, and the doing, undoing, and doing again that anyone who's been there would recognize.

For example, early one morning I drove past a house and the thought hit me that the smoke I saw might be from a fire. I drove a little further, assuring myself this was highly unlikely, but then *I had to go back*, to be certain, as much for the good of the people in that house as to protect myself from the possible guilt of not having intervened to save their lives. Even after I was sure it was only chimney smoke, I still had to go back again. And then, after everything was said and done, I chastised myself for not having the willpower to stifle the impression in the first place.

I was probably within an eyelash of insanity as I tried to protect my damaged emotions by not doing any more "bad" things. But no matter what standards I set, I failed, because had I achieved "perfection" for one day—which never happened—I would have chastised myself for setting my standards too low, or taken pride in my achievement, an even more despicable outcome!

The sad fact was, *I needed to fail.* Success—any success—would have been too kind an outcome for as negligent a father as I. So, I spent a lot of my time apologizing—for actions, inactions, motives, attitudes—because I so desperately needed people telling me I was forgiven. Yet no number of such assurances could have released me from my own emotional prison, designed, constructed, and maintained by a brutal jailer, me.

Looking back, I wonder what would have happened if somebody had stepped into that cell with me and said, "I love you, Dave, and it breaks my heart to see the downward spiral of your struggle with guilt. If you want me to, I'll climb up on the church steeple and proclaim to the world: David's not guilty. Not guilty. NOT GUILTY! He didn't kill Jonathan. It was an accident!

"You see, Dave, that's what you've been forcing us all to do for months now, and I'd do it *for years* if it would really help. But you're not listening. We could declare your innocence until we were blue in the face, and you would refuse to let go of your guilt.

"So, let's look at this another way. Maybe, just between us two, we should face something: You *are* guilty. You let Jonathan down. You failed. That's what you really feel, isn't it? That's what you believe is true. So I'm going to sit here and cry with you about that and feel this as much as any man can share another man's heartache. And when there aren't any more tears, there's one other thing I hope you will accept: I forgive you, friend. You are forgiven."

Deadly Directions

Unfortunately, no interchange like this ever took place. Nobody ever really met me where I was, at least not for years. And even then, *nobody let me be guilty so I could be forgiven.*

Instead, the emotional confusion led to a deep and lengthy depression, beginning with unrelieved sadness and leading to a chronic depletion (emotional, physical, and spiritual) which only finally resolved with medical intervention. I had PTSD, only the battleground was my heart.

Not everyone who experiences a severe loss moves from normal grieving to real depressive illness. In fact, as Dr. George Nichols wrote in a letter to me, "Although grief is a highly individual and personal matter, most people recover slowly without special attention or treatment. It is only occasionally that a true depressive illness interrupts that recovery. The distinction is important because clinical depression can be fatal, and because it is highly curable with medical care and medicine.

"It is easy to spot a broken leg, but recognizing a depressive illness requires a little new knowledge, usually a little change in viewpoint, and the willingness to ask a few questions—questions that bring out the signs which determine whether a person has a depressive illness or not."

Dr. Nichols speaks from experience. His youngest son committed suicide, and after that the doctor dedicated himself to raising public awareness of this very common and unnecessarily deadly disease. His insights, published in the *Journal of the Christian Medical and Dental Society*, are my foundation for these "diagnostic" questions, which are not intended to replace a medical evaluation, but to assist you in determining how seriously your friend is troubled, since he or she may desperately need your intervention:

- How have you been feeling?
- Is anything really bothering you?
- Have you been out lately?
- What did you have for supper last night?
- When was the last time you laughed?
- Heard any good jokes lately?

- Any health problems you've never had before?

Listen very closely for these symptoms:

- Recurrent thoughts of death or suicide
- Sad, unhappy mood; but sometimes irritable and anxious (some people deny mood changes)
- Feelings of hopelessness, worthlessness, and self-reproach
- Crying, or inability to cry
- Withdrawal
- Loss of interest and of pleasure in things
- Neglect of personal appearance
- Difficulty in thinking and concentrating
- Sleeping problems: may have trouble falling asleep, but often awakens too early, or sleeps too much
- Change in appetite or weight
- Physical: slow and tired, or may be agitated and restless
- Complaints of physical ill health: e.g., fast heartbeat, headache, constipation, chronic pain. (Symptoms like these are common, but misleading, and disguise the underlying sadness; they probably mean that the person is worried about himself and is asking for help in approved—non-emotional—words.)

Most of us have some of these symptoms at times. But if your heartbroken friend has them in combinations, or if they persist, the best help you can offer is to make a doctor's appointment for her or him, and then go along. This is *extremely* urgent if the following signs are also present:

- Increasing distance and withdrawal from family and friends
- Absence of hope
- Hearing voices and other disordered thinking
- Talking of suicide
- Giving away prized possessions—e.g., trophies, hi-fi and sports equipment, baseball cards; "I won't be needing these anymore"
- Putting affairs in order—e.g., returning long-borrowed items; final contact (unspoken goodbyes) with important friends and relatives
- Sudden improvement (no longer painfully undecided).

Immediate intervention is crucial if you want to help your friend *survive*, much less recover. If you really care, you'll put your arm around him or her and say, "I love you, and because I do we're going to the doctor to get some help for what's got you down."

When I was about as low as I ever got, a physician-friend said, "I've known you for quite a while, Dave. But I've never seen you this down. Maybe you should consider medication; specifically, Prozac."

I couldn't deny the depression, though I doubt I knew how bad it was. And I did trust my friend, even if I resented his intrusion. But still I resisted, probably because of the stigma of needing the pharmacological crutch. I told him I would follow up when I got home, but I battled it for several more months until pneumonia drained my last reserves and I had no other choice but to use every crutch I could find if I ever wanted to be whole again.

That was April 1991, and the one symptom I remember that

seems to symbolize everything else was that even the sound of the birds singing outside each morning that spring—thirteen years after Jonathan died—irritated me. The next spring I actually enjoyed their music! Hopefully, every spring that follows will increase my ability to experience nature's music as the symphony it really is, rather than the cacophony I heard in 1991, when it was still hard to believe that I would ever again be anything but sad.

For Reflection or Discussion

1. Most of Rocky's emotionally laden questions began with Why? As a group, make a list of what these questions might have been.

2. Glenn's answer to Rocky's agony was to hold him and cry with him. How does this response compare to the kind of help usually offered by Christians to their heartbroken friends? [Note: I once had a pastor cancel, at the last minute, my speaking engagement because he thought Glenn's effort to help Rocky was inappropriate. What do you think about that?]

3. Have someone in your group represent Betsy, who has withdrawn in depression from just about everybody. Have one of Betsy's former friends visit her, with the goal of convincing her that her reaction is a bad witness. After the visit is over, let the role players express their feelings about the interaction, and then discuss as a group what might have been more helpful.

4. What do you think of Betsy's desire for "Christ in the form

of people to show me he/they cared"?

- ❏ Impossible
- ❏ Unreasonable
- ❏ Unlikely
- ❏ Possible, but difficult
- ❏ Natural
- ❏ Piece of cake
- ❏ Is this some kind of visualization exercise?
- ❏ Other:

5. Have you ever experienced an extreme emotional reaction because the event in question has tapped some hurtful memory? If so, and you wish to do so, share it with the group.
    How can your friends help you toward healing of that memory?

6. If many believers know all they need to know in order to survive, why do so many of them suffer so deeply with heartbreak?

    - ❏ It's part of being human
    - ❏ It's disobedient and only makes things worse
    - ❏ Ideas aren't very helpful in times like that
    - ❏ Heartbreak is a lonely road
    - ❏ Nobody cares enough to help them

7. If you've experienced heartbreak, what approaches did people use to try to help you?

8. Why is the idea of entering the emotional open door so crucial if you want to really connect with your hurting friend? Discuss how to find these open doors.

9. Is your friend struggling with guilt, even though nobody else blames her or him for what has happened? If so, would it help to say, "Okay, maybe you are guilty, but I forgive you"? How would you go about it? What dangers might there be in this approach? (Hint: If your friend is suicidal, it probably won't help much to remind him or her that he or she is guilty.)

10. Review the list of symptoms of depression and develop your own questions to discern where your friend is in relation to this. Where is the line between normal grief and clinical depression?

11. Is there a stigma attached to seeing a psychiatrist for depression? How about taking medication for treatment of depression? If the group's answer is yes to either of these, discuss why this may be true and what a more helpful attitude might be. How might even a subtle agreement with this viewpoint affect your ability to really help a clinically depressed friend?

12. Choose one of the following passages and discuss how Jesus entered the person's "open door" of need:
    - ❑ The woman at the well (John 4:7-26)
    - ❑ The adulterous woman (John 8:1-11)
    - ❑ Lazarus resurrected (John 11:1-45)
    - ❑ The road to Emmaus (Luke 24:13-35)
    - ❑ Mary in the garden (John 20:11-18)

13. Draw three intersecting circles on the board, labeling them emotions, mind, and will. This diagram represents the personality (or soul). Discuss the implications of the intersections in relation to helping a person recover.

14. What emotions does God have? If we are made "in his image," does that include an emotional component of our personality?

15. List all the emotions of Jesus you can find in the Gospels, such as anger, discouragement, confusion, grief, depression, joy. Are there any hidden values to being an emotional person? How can you help a heartbroken friend capitalize on these?

16. Based on the biblical survey of God's emotions you've just done, how would you compare the way human emotions are presented in the Bible:
    - ❏ normal and natural
    - ❏ a hindrance to spirituality
    - ❏ an avenue to closeness with God
    - ❏ neutral

    In light of this, how would you evaluate the Christian teaching you've received about emotions?

Chapter 9

To tell the truth

Give your friend the freedom to not pretend.

Like many alcoholics, Billy Simpson started drinking heavily when he was in college. The university's football team was exciting to watch, so Billy and his friend John had to get to the stadium at least three hours before game time, just to get a seat in the student section.

To pass the time, they smuggled in alcohol—starting with a pint they would share. Gradually, they needed more booze to get the same buzz. By the time they quit going to football games together, Billy and John were packing three quarts of hard liquor to every game.

Billy Simpson dropped out of college halfway through his sophomore year, moved home, and got a job reading meters—which he's still doing today. He also married his first wife, Donna, as soon as she finished high school.

Billy and Donna partied, drank, did drugs, and got along reasonably well for about a year—until Donna became pregnant. Billy was unwilling to face the responsibilities of a family, so he turned, increasingly, to drinking and womanizing.

Like many alcoholics, Billy Simpson had a Jekyll and Hyde personality when he was drinking. "I could be talking to a friend, being completely normal, in front of a store," he said, "and the next minute kick in the window and take things out."

When Billy's first marriage ended in divorce, he married his second wife, Shelly, *the very next day*. "It was good for maybe six months," he said. "Then the same pattern returned. I started going out on her and drinking more, mainly at home, from about 5:30 p.m. until I passed out between 12:30 and 1 a.m."

Finally, Shelly convinced Billy to see a doctor, who at seventy-five had seen many men like Billy. "He ran a batch of tests," Billy said, "and told me I was an alcoholic. My liver was about shot and a lot of my bodily functions were starting to shut down.

"'If you don't quit,' he told me, 'you're going to kill yourself.'"

Shelly wouldn't let Billy kill himself. Two months later, Billy entered a program, and he stayed sober for about a year. But on their wedding anniversary, he had a couple of drinks with dinner, six or more the next day, and a whole quart on the third. He stopped drinking again when Shelly warned, "I've had it with you. If you mess up again, you're out of here. I'll give you one more chance."

This time Billy stayed on the wagon for fifteen months, but he always knew he would drink again, someday, if only to test Shelly's limits. The final episode lasted nearly four months until, on New Year's Day, Shelly told Billy they were finished.

Although it took her several months to get him out of the house, Billy finally got the point. He's been sober since that day, not so much by his own power, but because as he tried to recover from his second marriage failure, someone introduced him to Christ.

At a church's divorce recovery workshop, he met Brenda (whose daughter, Celeste, cut her face—see chapter 6). Billy and Brenda have built a new life together, in which Billy's grandchildren don't even know the person he once was, but only the person he is becoming with God's help and Brenda's support. Today, because he regrets the misery he caused so many when he was drinking, Billy tries to help others in similar straits face and deal with the truth of their lives before they create their own legacy of broken hearts.

No Corner on Denial

If you were raised in the church like I was, you may think the Billy Simpsons of the world are "out there" somewhere. Not very often do people stand up *in church* (like they do in A.A.) and say, "My name is Billy, and I'm an alcoholic. But, thank God, I've stopped running from the pain."

Yet, Billy's journey is similar to that of many brokenhearted believers—not because they choose alcohol as an escape, but because *they choose denial in one form or another as a way of coping with their disappointments.*

Encouraged by a group of codependents who tell each other only what they want to hear when adversity happens (to reduce *their own* anxiety), the typical heartbroken Christian processes the pain in one of the following ways:

- Stoicism—This doesn't really hurt.
- Masochism—Hurting is good for me.
- Quietism—Who am I to question the will of God?
- Activism—I will rise above this.

When a person is aboard an airplane and experiences motion sickness, what he or she really needs to do is throw up. By analogy, when fellow travelers on the journey of faith experience vertigo, they're either told the turbulence isn't really that bad, or they're handed a scopolamine patch so they won't remember it, or a Dramamine tablet so they won't feel it. But seldom, if ever, do they receive what they really need, a spiritual air sickness bag.

Jeremy and Toni (see chapter 3) spent years trying to find somebody who would let them be who they were so they could become what they wanted to be. "Many who come to the church do not find healing because the problems they bring do not yield easily to current ideas about victory in Christ and so they tend to be ignored," Jeremy wrote. "My heart aches for the multitudes that the church has been unable to help. The first great enemy to lasting change is our propensity to turn our eyes away from the wound and pretend things are fine. *This, to me, is lying about the truth!* The work of restoration cannot begin until a problem is fully faced.

"There is a journey we must undertake if we are to become fully healed of a painful, ugly past," he continued. "The journey involves bringing our wounded heart before God, a heart that might be full of rage, overwhelmed with doubt, and unable to fellowship intimately with God. It does not seem possible that anyone (even God) can handle, let alone embrace, our wounded and sinful heart. But the pathway to healing involves the risk of putting into words the condition of our inner being and placing those words before God for his response."

Going Through It to Get Beyond It

After the doctors detected brain damage in our second son, Christopher, I cried out from the depths of my soul, "If that's the way it's going to be, then God can go to h—." Some reviewers of the manuscript that described that ordeal viewed my outburst as blasphemous. I think it was the cry of a brokenhearted child trying to verbalize to his Father a hurt that almost defied words. Only a few hours later, this gracious God shined the light of his hope into the darkness of my despair when I realized that he had already gone to hell, in the person of Jesus, to redeem this fallen world of which my sons' illnesses are a part and to redeem a fallen person who would dare to utter such a phrase.

Looking back, that kind of truthful interchange—me with God, and he with me—was what brought me through the experience and made me stronger. In fact, my verbal transparency before him, which on the level of words only may sound so outrageous to the human ear, on another level became evidence to me that our relationship was secure enough that I could risk telling God whatever I needed to.

If I had played the denial game, including saying and doing only the "right" things, I might have consigned myself to a prison of bitter resentment, ruining any chance that I would be able to fulfill what I now see as my calling, "to make a defense to everyone who asks you to give an account for the hope that is in you, yet with gentleness and reverence" (1 Pet. 3:15, NASB).

Pain (especially psychic or spiritual pain) *is* profane, and if your heartbroken friend is ever going to get beyond it, you'll have to let her label it any way she likes. There's a similarity here between this process and how many people face illness. Their first reaction is to ignore or deny it, as if by waiting the problem will resolve. Often, thankfully, this does happen.

But in terms of certain diseases, notably certain cancers, denial can be deadly. The symptoms must be faced, and once a person decides to do that, it doesn't make any sense or do any good to get into the examining room and act like nothing's wrong. Of course, most physicians will refuse to accept denial as truth, relentlessly probing your symptoms and history, searching for clues until both of you arrive at the only thing that will help—a label that describes your reality. Treating the symptoms might help, even without a label. But giving the problem a name is the only way to really pursue an effective treatment and cure.

In a similar way, pretending never helped a broken-hearted person become whole again. No responsible soul doctor will support that approach, since only telling the truth can begin the process of healing. But what if, in telling the truth, your brokenhearted friend insists on saying things that are irreverent, or worse? Well then, rejoice; not in her impiety, but in her willingness to entrust her pain to you.

For instance, many Christians are angry at God for either causing or allowing the event that has stolen their joy and broken their dreams. If your friend feels this way, and trusts you enough, don't be surprised to hear, "I'm so mad I could spit. I thought God loved me, but not even somebody who hated me could hurt me more than this," and so on.

If you're ever privileged to hear honesty like this, you'll be as close to representing God as is humanly possible. So your response is extremely important, not only to your friend but to God. In responding, remember Jesus, who, as he hung on the Cross, absorbing the hatred and abuse of those who put him there, said, "Father, forgive them, they don't know what they're doing."

You can bring this forgiveness into your friend's confusion by affirming the sentiments as legitimate expressions of her perspective at this point in time. For instance, you might say, "I've been disappointed sometimes, and even been angry with God for the way things have worked out. I worried about it at first, but then I realized my feelings couldn't possibly take him by surprise. Not only that, some people in the Bible, like Moses, got pretty upset with God sometimes. So I wasn't the first person, and you're not the last one, to feel that way toward him."

Expect One of Three Responses

If you'll do this, sincerely, instead of trying to correct your friend's thinking, she will likely choose one of three directions. She might say, "Really? How did you get over it?" In this case, you could explain that when we have a problem with another human person the best way to keep it from turning into bitterness that defiles and enslaves us is to confront, confess, forgive, and be reconciled. Reconciling with God—the ultimate Person—means expressing the truth about how we feel and view things, including his role, and choosing to lay aside the anger, resentment, and bitterness so they will not further hinder our ability to love him. *When she's ready*, you might offer to be her witness in the prayer she will need to pray in order to find release and reconciliation.

By contrast, she might say, "Maybe you worked it out, but I'm not interested. It's just totally, absolutely, and eternally unfair. I don't care what you, God, or anybody in between tries to make me think or say!"

If this is her response, again, rejoice, not because she insists on wallowing in her pain but because she's willing to state her case without pretense. This gift of extreme vulnerability should be cherished and never treated with contempt by telling someone else what's been said.

In order to help your friend, your biggest battle may not be with her—after all, you're trying to be her ally—but with *yourself*. The more you love your friend, the more her insistence on remaining in the prison of her own making will hurt you, because you long for her to find her way to freedom.

Regardless of how strong your inclinations are to intervene, don't, don't, don't try to "make her think or say" *anything* at this point. She may be testing you, to see whose agenda is really most important. She must discover if the love you represent (your own and God's) is real before her trust can be renewed.

If there's any principle involved, it's to consider doing the opposite of what your religious training or personal inclinations seem to suggest, because most of the more common approaches are aimed at releasing *the helper* in one way or another.

Stifle all your aspirations but one—to be an agent of grace in the midst of your friend's pain, patiently and prayerfully watching for the opportunity to introduce a flicker of hope into the dungeon of her despair.

In *Pilgrim's Progress*, at one point Christian and his companion, Hope, are captured by Giant Despair and thrown into the dungeon of Doubting Castle. They languish there until Christian remembers, "What a fool I am to lie stinking in a dungeon when I may walk at liberty. I have a key in my bosom called Promise that I am persuaded will open any lock in Doubting Castle."[1]

Christian's key—Promise—was there all the time, but *he had to remember it was there*. This is the third possible response your friend could make, and you can facilitate it by being her faithful companion in that cell.

When Giant Despair inquired why they should "choose to live when their lives were attended by such bitterness," Christian turned to Hope and said, "Brother, what shall we do? The life we now live is miserable. For my part, I do not know whether it is better to live this way or to die by our own hand. My soul chooses strangling rather than life, and the grave is easier for me than the dungeon. Shall we be ruled by the giant?"

> *If there's any principle involved, it's to consider doing the opposite of what your religious training or personal inclinations seem to suggest.*

Hope's answer is refreshing in its honesty: "Indeed, our present condition is dreadful, and death would be far more welcome than abiding this way forever.... [But] others have been taken by Giant Despair and have escaped. I am resolved to be patient and endure awhile and to try my utmost to get from under his hand."[2]

You don't have to force your friend to sing jolly tunes in order to help her free herself from the dungeon of Doubting Castle. You just need to follow Hope's 300-plus-year-old example: Validate reality, but encourage your friend to keep looking for a way out.

The Key Is a Person

God's *promises* unlock every door in the castle of Despair. And, as 2 Corinthians 1:20 makes clear, all God's promises are

"Yes" in Christ. Jesus, the Promised One—whose life, death, and resurrection point the way beyond even the most abject human pain—is the Divine antidote to brokenness, able to guard both heart and mind (see Phil. 4:6-9).

How does he do it? First of all, he always tells the truth. And just as importantly, he speaks the truth in love.

As Jeremy reminded me, Jesus never forced his view of truth on anybody, because he "knew that a godly man (or woman) is *built*, line upon line, precept upon precept and that *only* the Holy Spirit can reveal God's truth to a person in a life-changing way, though seeds are often planted through the lives of others.

"Therefore," he added, "if I try to cram 'truth' down another person's throat to avoid personal suffering I am only prolonging the process of growth and maturity in that person—the *opposite* of what is needed. This is why some people are never truly and completely healed. The brothers and sisters around them aren't strong enough spiritually to endure with them long enough. Instead, most people end up trying to *act* healed in order to be accepted and loved."

In the previous chapter we looked at how Jesus might minister to the emotions of heartbreak. But how would he approach the mental confusion that also usually goes with it?

He would ask questions.

For instance, he might ask:

- Can you change what's happened?
- Did you do everything you could?
- Are there others who need you?
- Do you really want to be healed?
- Can you still believe that God loves you?

He would tell a story. I created this fractured fairy tale not only to get a laugh, but to make a point:

> Once upon a time there was a beautiful princess, who lived with her father the king in their fairyland kingdom, where all was sweetness and light, and everyone lived happily ever after. Except for one thing. The princess was lonely, and often when she was lonely she would sit gazing into the reflecting pool by the side of the castle, wondering what would become of her and how she would ever meet the handsome prince of her dreams.
>
> One day, while gazing into the pool, she noticed a frog sitting on a lily pad, a frog that seemed to be gazing at her, too. Now the princess was well versed in fairy tales, and she knew that sometimes evil spells were cast, turning handsome princes into frogs, and she began to think perhaps that this frog might be just such a prince in disguise.
>
> Well, after many visits to the beautiful pool, and many encounters with this particular frog, the princess had finally made up her mind, and one day, she reached into the water, caught the frog and before she could change her mind, she kissed it, which she knew was the only way to liberate the prince from the spell.
>
> Unfortunately for this particular princess, that kiss immediately transformed her into a frog and she spent the rest of her days serenading the palace guards.

The point? Fairy tales don't always come with happy endings. Life is full of unhappy surprises.

He would use symbols. Jeremy did this with one of his friends whose direction had become a serious concern. He sent him an old photo, and a little note: "Remember these two guys? They used to be real close." The message behind the message was: "I love you. I've been hanging on to you tooth and nail for twelve or thirteen years, man. But who are we really, now?"

He would use music. Although there's no biblical record of Jesus singing, I am confident that, despite Barry Manilow's claims to the contrary, *Jesus* is music; he writes the songs—especially the songs that bridge the gap between the heart and mind. Sometimes music can find an entrance that words can't, because music speaks to the emotions and spirit as well as to the mind.

For Reflection or Discussion

1. If you have tried to work with alcoholics in the past, describe some of the difficulties, as well as some approaches that worked. If Billy were your friend, how would you have tried to intervene before he messed up the lives of so many other people?

2. Billy admitted that he went on his last binge to test Shelly's limits. Do you think she was justified in kicking him out? What do you think of her timing (New Year's Day)? Have two group participants role-play the New Year's Day interchange between Shelly and Billy. After they finish, debrief as a group, and see if you can think of any way to rescue this marriage.

3. How did you react to my outburst, "If that's the way it's going to be, then God can go to h___!"

    ❏ Honest, but extreme

- ❏ Blasphemy
- ❏ I wouldn't want my kids to read this
- ❏ I wouldn't risk it, myself
- ❏ Human, but not very spiritual
- ❏ A key to his future healing
- ❏ This question isn't fair

4. Suppose your friend has just said, "I'm so mad at God I could spit!" Can you see how hearing this kind of honesty is a privilege and "as close to representing God as is humanly possible?" How would you respond?

5. What does it mean to be "an agent of grace"?

6. Evaluate Jeremy's comments in relation to "lying about the truth." Is he right that there are multitudes the church hasn't been able to reach because of this "propensity to turn our eyes away from the wound and pretend things are fine"? Create and role-play a situation where this kind of denial is common.

7. Make up a fairy tale or story that summarizes your own journey with heartbreak. Share it with the group.

8. As a group, create a list of questions that might lead a person toward seeing the truth about the way he is handling his heartbreak.

9. Discuss the role music can have—positive or negative—in helping people recover from loss. If a particular song has ministered to you in this regard, share it with the group.

10. Read Philippians 4:6-9 and discuss the difference between the *peace of God* and the *God of peace*, and how

knowing Jesus in a personal sense can introduce a peace that is able to guard both heart and mind. What is the key here, and how are both sides of this equation important in the journey of a heartbroken person toward wholeness?

Chapter 10

Moving with the pain

Your friend may need a birthing coach.

Anybody who could move away from a crowded, polluted, crime-infested metropolitan area to Colorado to work with a rapidly growing international Christian ministry with apparently limitless potential would be completely excited and eternally grateful, right?

Not necessarily. At least not Martha, who had struggled all her life with feelings of deprivation and abandonment. Her parents loved each other so much, Martha (an only child) felt excluded. Just after she married Bruce, who seemed so dependable, the problems they were facing got so overwhelming, he left for a while. With time they worked things out, and built a happy home. But then Bruce died and Martha was left to raise two children, ages five and ten, who had their own sets of problems.

Martha buried herself in her work and kept "a cotton batting" around her emotional self until many years later she was able to live in the same home with her grandchildren for a while. With them she developed a two-way love that was more free and secure and beautiful than anything she had ever experienced or imagined.

But then her company moved a thousand miles. Perhaps because she had a year's advance notice, the agony of leaving those little girls didn't really hit Martha until the weekend she moved into her new townhouse in Colorado. Suddenly all those old feelings of desertion, abandonment, and fear let loose, far more intensely than she had expected.

"My first weekend here," she said, "was a three-day weekend, which I spent crying at the top of my lungs and shaking my fist at God and saying, 'I can't do this. I can't live through this. Why should you make me do this? Why would you let this happen?'

"I wondered, *Is it ever going to stop? Is this ever going to get better? Who can I call that will tell me when it stops hurting? When do I stop feeling like I'm all raw and torn apart?*"

There were several factors in Martha's recovery. The first was that God did not leave her alone in Colorado, but brought a new and very special friend into her life . . . Katherine, who understood her pain and was willing to walk through it with her.

But nearly as important was a choice Martha made about the way she would look at her situation. With time she realized her anxieties were driven by the fear that God might leave her, too.

Insight, however, wasn't enough. It never is. In order for Martha to transform a heartbreaking loss into an opportunity for growth, she had to make a conscious choice to view her situation differently. Instead of continuing to focus only on what she had lost, she began looking for what she might gain by trusting God instead of questioning him.

"He showed me that he chose to make that separation so I

could learn not to be dependent on anybody, or any situation, but only on him," Martha said. "I'm working toward that. It is not an easy thing. Sometimes I take two steps forward, and three back—but overall I'm making progress. Little by little, he's healing that fear of being alone and teaching me that Jim Elliot's perspective was right, 'You're never less alone than when you're alone with God.'

"So that's what I'm trying to learn during this time. I believe eventually that my son-in-law will find a job out here, and we'll be close again," she added. "But I don't think it will happen until I'm dependent on God instead of the people in my life. The good thing about that is that when our family's together again, our relationships will be healthier, too."

Choices . . . Changes

Many heartbroken people get stuck in a vain effort to change what has occurred so life can return to "normal"—the way things used to be. But no situation can ever be the way it used to be. As the old proverb says, "You can't step in the same river twice." You'll get wet enough, but the water you stepped in before is now somewhere downstream.

When the loss comes through terminal illness, this struggle can be doubly difficult since the "goodbye" begins while the dying one is still alive and continues long after they're gone. To the grieving mind, it seems that anything other than clinging to what might have been seems disloyal to the deceased, especially if he was a child.

Dan, a pastor for many years, had numerous opportunities to help families change the way they were approaching crisis. The case that symbolized the rest was a four-year-old leukemia victim we'll call Jimmy.

Jimmy went through several remissions and relapses, an experience shared by the church. "We were on an emotional roller coaster for months," Dan recalled. "It was eating Jimmy's parents alive, along with his grandmother and some aunts and uncles who were part of the church.

"Toward the end, when Jimmy was failing, I went to call on the family. It was a long drive so all the way, I prayed. *Lord, give me wisdom. I don't know what to say, but I really want to help.*

"When I got there, we passed the time of day for a little bit," Dan said, "and then I got serious with them and I said, 'I came with a very strange request tonight. I know that it's nothing you've ever heard before, but, because I care, I want to help you. I've come tonight to ask you to give Jimmy to God.'

"You could have heard a pin drop for a long time. I didn't say anything; I just let them think about it awhile. Finally, I said, 'Through these years, we've prayed many times for Jimmy, and now it's apparent that probably God is not going to heal him. So I'd like for you to just place him in God's hands and trust God with the outcome. Do you think you could do that?'

"Jimmy's parents looked at each other, and began to cry. Then his mother said, 'I could do that.' And his father said, 'I can, too.'

"So I prayed with them, and it was a pretty heavy evening. I tried to leave them on a positive note—that if they had committed Jimmy to God, then they could trust God with him. That was on Saturday. The following Tuesday night, late, I got a phone call that Jimmy was in the children's hospital in Denver; would I come?

"About midnight, it was obvious the boy wasn't going to make it. I'll never forget walking with that father to the end of the hall where there was a big window. He looked me straight in the eye, and said, 'Pastor, I meant what I said Saturday night. I gave him to God. My commitment's still the same tonight; I just want you to know that.' I sensed that already he was beginning to heal. He already had something to lean on when Jimmy died.

"Then we went back into the room, and he put his arm around his wife and said the same thing to her, and she reaffirmed it. Well, within forty-five minutes, their little boy was gone. But they were prepared, and already beginning to work into their grief. It wasn't so much that I was with them—though I believe God helped me help them. But what really helped them was that they consciously turned it over to God. Through this choice, they were saying, 'We're taking control of this situation by putting it in God's hands.'"

Facilitate Without Forcing

There are many paradoxes of faith, but this is one of the greatest—the way to gain control is by giving it to God. There are other similar paradoxes in the Scriptures, many of which can be related to recovering from loss:

- We're wisest when we admit our foolishness.
- The way to gain real life is to lose our life in his.
- The way to wholeness is through being broken.
- We're strongest when we give our weakness to him.

Remember the apostle Paul's experience with his "thorn in the flesh"? God's message to him was, "My grace is sufficient for you, for power is perfected in weakness." So, Paul says, "I am well content with weaknesses, with insults, with distresses, with persecutions, with difficulties, for Christ's sake; for when I am weak, then I am strong" (2 Corinthians 12:9-10, NASB).

The paradoxes of God are enigmatic to the human mind, which wants to control, overcome, and win. But God's consistent message (through both Old and New Testaments) is "the way to overcome is to give the control to me."

In the Garden of Gethsemane, the night he was betrayed, Jesus agonized with his fate to the point of—according to Dr. Luke—sweating blood. "Father," Jesus prayed, "if Thou art willing, remove this cup from Me; yet not My will, but Thine be done" (Luke 22:42 NASB).

When our son Jonathan became ill, we didn't know how to pray. We were too confused in heart and mind. Someone suggested that "Thy will be done" seemed rather passive in a situation like that. Through the lens of going on forty years, however, those words have taken on increasing meaning and power.

> There are many paradoxes of faith, but this is one of the greatest—the way to gain control is by giving it to God.

To pray, "My will be done, regardless," is the epitome of unfaith. To pray, "Heal our son, according to thy will" is the essence of trust, because it leaves the power where it really lies . . . in the hands of God, which reduces our need to ensure any particular result

Don't misunderstand me. I would have died in Jonathan's place, had God given me that choice. But the only choice I really had was whether or not I would embrace God's way with him (and with us) rather than insisting on my own way.

Brokenhearted believers always face this choice: Will I hold on to the pain or consciously choose to give it all to God, by faith, trusting that—

- He knows what he is doing;
- He is motivated by love in everything he causes or allows;
- He really does understand the way I feel.

Long before his agony in the Garden, Jesus had "steadfastly set his face to go to Jerusalem," knowing full well what would happen there. Long before that choice, he chose to become a human being, to enter our pain for the purpose of redeeming it—and us—for the glory of God. Even before that, in the council of the Almighty, he had been chosen to die, the "Lamb slain before the foundation of the world." In other words, before creating mankind, God already knew that, by creating us with freedom to choose, he was writing his own death sentence.

So God knows about heartbreak, from the pain of creating beings he knew would reject him, to the grief of watching his own Son die. As the Suffering Servant:

> He was despised and forsaken of men,
> A man of sorrows, and acquainted with grief . . .
> Surely our griefs He Himself bore,
> And our sorrows He carried . . .
> He was pierced through for our transgressions,
> He was crushed for our iniquities;
> The chastening for our well-being fell upon Him,
> And by His scourging we are healed.
> (Isa. 53:3-5, NASB)

Jesus fully entered our reality, becoming our great High Priest who understands our weaknesses because he was "tempted in all things as we are, yet without sin. Let us therefore draw near with confidence to the throne of grace, that we may receive mercy and may find grace to help in time of need" (from Heb. 4:15-16 NASB).

God hurts when we hurt. When you ache with your brokenhearted friend, you emulate the *heart* of God. When you long to communicate truth to your friend as an anchor for her soul, you emulate the *mind* of God. But when you help her choose to work with God to redeem the pain for his glory, only the *method* of God can produce the desired result. God never forces anyone to trust him. It is his *kindness*, not his power or even his persuasiveness, that leads to repentance.

If God will never force your heartbroken friend to embrace his way, you must resist any tendency to push for resolution. As long as you force, your friend will resist. But if you love God enough, you'll entrust the outcome to him. And *if you love your friend enough*, you'll set her free to choose.

There's a risk involved—she may choose contrary to what you know is best for her. She may turn away from faith. She may even turn away from you. But if this happens, you'll have an opportunity to understand the heartbreak of God when the race created in his own image chose against him (and continues to do so).

Discernment, wisdom, timing, sensitivity, and faith are essential here, perhaps more than at any other point in your journey with your friend through heartbreak toward wholeness. And prayer is the key to all of them, because what's really happening is spiritual in nature—a warfare for your friend's soul—in which the outcome is in doubt until she decides which way she will move with the pain.

Your role will be like that of a birth coach, whose function is to help a woman in labor use the pain properly, in a process that leads through agony to joy. Sometimes the coach says "pant and blow" to counteract the contractions, because pushing too early would only hurt the baby as well as the mother. Between contractions, the coach may offer some ice chips and a cool, damp towel to wipe the woman's brow. But the coach's crucial role is supportive—another person willing to share the mother's pain—until the marvelous moment when it's time to push that baby into the hands of the waiting doctor or midwife.

If you've ever given birth with the help of a coach, you'll understand immediately the value of having that objective person involved. Your heartbroken friend has a similar need, since there are times when the pain is so great and the experience so exhausting it is nearly impossible to gain a realistic perspective on what's happening.

Coffin or Cocoon

Recently I saw an interview with a mother whose nine-year-old daughter's murder is still unsolved. Even eight months after the funeral, the mother hasn't changed the girl's room. She made it clear that she will *never* change it.

Grief like this will be either a coffin or a cocoon. If it's a coffin, the epitaph will read: "Died at thirty, buried at seventy." If it's a cocoon, someday a new creation will emerge, far more beautiful than any broken person dreamed of becoming.

Every heartbroken person faces this predicament. Which will it be—coffin or cocoon? Both are painful, involving a "death" of sorts. The former is easier, since its primary focus is the past. Hurtful as the experience may have been, it is still more comfortable to cling to the known than to launch into the unknown. But choosing to spin the cocoon is far more constructive, despite its risks. Flying gracefully through the air is always better than rotting from the inside out.

Metamorphosis is where God is going in your friend's life, but you can't force her to cooperate. You can only help her choose. Here are some suggestions:

- Ask her to identify her most important issues. Once the list exists, ask her to choose one she wants to do something about and then work with her on this one thing until it is resolved. Then go on to the next one *she wants to tackle*. Hint: Don't force her to prioritize the list and work on the hardest things first. Baby steps forward are better than regression.

- Help her focus on positive things, at least once a day, by sending cards, leaving notes, calling, or in many other creative ways. You're helping her fulfill Philippians 4:8: "Whatever is true . . . honorable . . . right . . . pure . . . lovely . . . of good repute, if there is any excellence and if anything worthy of praise, let your mind dwell on these things" (NASB). The ultimate healing focus for the mind is in worship and praise—so when she's ready you might invite her along with you to church. Even before that, you could provide her with musical tapes and other uplifting materials.

- Look for and discuss situations in the news (or some other neutral setting) like the mother who refuses to change her murdered daughter's room. For instance, you might comment, "She must have really loved her daughter. Can a person ever recover from something like that?" This could lead—but don't force it—to the importance of choices, perspectives, and other issues mentioned in this chapter. If it does, you might ask: "Where do you want to be in five years—or three years, or even next year?" Or when she's ready, ask, "What do you think God wants (or expects) of you in relation to this experience?"

- Remember—and communicate to her—that metamorphosis is gradual, not an instantaneous change. Accepting this will impact your patience quotient—as well as your friend's expectations of herself.

Nancy Miller was working as an interpreter at a Mennonite hospital in Haiti when her three-day-old son died.

She wrote, "I had a real tough time because I had no one who had experienced the death of a child. I felt I should be finished with my grieving after a week."

Instead of seven days, however, Nancy's grieving lasted seven *years*, until she finally faced her anger at God. Thankfully, having resolved it, she has been able to use the experience to minister to others. "I was trying to help a mother who had a handicapped child," she wrote. "I asked her if she might be angry with God. She replied, 'No, you can't get angry with God.' I helped her see God was very capable of handling our anger and she said, 'Yes, I am angry at God. My father was an alcoholic, my mother is in a mental institution, and now I have a handicapped child.' We worked through the anger process and she became a different mother. A couple of weeks later I heard her ask another mother, 'Are you angry at God? You know you can be—God can handle your anger—Mrs. Miller was, and she's a Mennonite!'"

Share stories like this one with your friend, using them to help her move beyond her anger toward the reconciliations that must take place—with God, others, and herself—if she is to become whole. As she moves in that direction, she will be participating in what Peter Kreeft calls "spiritual judo"—using the enemy's force against him.

This has happened for Theresa, who described her life as one "filled with overwhelming amounts and types of pain . . . child abuse/molestation, never-ending ridicule, the loss of many friends (I couldn't change my outlook on life according to their timetable), the deaths of both of my parents and two very special aunts (all within a two-year period), physical disability in both legs, then a back injury which has caused pain beyond description, lung disorders, clinical depression, and more."

But Theresa adds, "Physically, I hurt, but spiritually, I'm becoming stronger in faith, increasing in hope, and developing my love for others. Currently, my ministry includes face-painting for children during outreaches, learning guitar, and singing. I love the Lord and am really learning that he loves me, too!"

For Reflection or Discussion

1. How would you have tried to help Martha during her first long weekend of separation from her family, which she spent crying at the top of her lungs and shaking her fist at God?
    - ❏ By saying, "Get a grip on it, Martha. My goodness, You're a grown woman."
    - ❏ By sitting with her and trying to understand her pain.
    - ❏ By inviting her out to a local comedy club.
    - ❏ By calling all her friends and asking them to pray for her.
    - ❏ By having her over to my house for a quiet dinner.
    - ❏ By leaving her alone so she could get it out.

❑ Other:

2. In Martha's case, insight was important in motivating her choice of how to approach this brokenness. Put into your own words what insight helped her, and recall any similar experiences you have had.

3. Is your present position where you want to be in three years? If not, what choices must you make in order to move in a more desirable direction?

4. Evaluate Pastor Dan's approach to Jimmy's parents. How did you respond when you read his words, "I've come tonight to ask you to give Jimmy to God"?

   ❑ He was misinformed about God's promise to heal.
   ❑ He was just trying to get it off his own mind.
   ❑ His guidance helped them to be more realistic.
   ❑ His involvement showed them the path toward their own healing.
   ❑ It was just a mind game in the end. What difference did it really make?
   ❑ Other:

5. Discuss the "paradoxes of faith" concept and make a list of any biblical teachings or examples that support the idea that the ways of God are often the opposite of what human beings would choose. To get you started, here are a few, some of them mentioned in the text:

   ❑ The way to gain control is to give it to God.
   ❑ We're strongest when we give our weakness to God.
   ❑ We're wisest when we admit our foolishness.

- ❑ We're richest when we've become poor for his sake.
- ❑ The way to be exalted is to humble yourself.
- ❑ The way to gain life is to lose it.
- ❑ The way to be first is to be last.
- ❑ The way to gain authority is to become a servant.

6. Is praying "Not my will, but thine be done" a passive approach or a difficult, conscious choice? Is there any difference between this prayer and "Heal our son, according to thy will"? Share experiences you have had with this.

7. Which of these assertions is the hardest to accept in the face of a devastating experience?
    - ❑ God knows what he is doing;
    - ❑ God is motivated by love in everything he causes or allows;
    - ❑ God really does understand the way I feel.

8. Support (or challenge) the idea that God hurts when we hurt. How might believing this be helpful to a brokenhearted person?

9. How does the knowledge that Jesus "was tempted in all things as we are, yet without sin" increase your confidence in coming to the throne of grace in time of need?
    - ❑ It doesn't, since he never sinned.
    - ❑ Not too much, but I do it anyway.
    - ❑ Quite a lot, because mercy is most valuable from one who has walked in shoes a lot like mine.
    - ❑ Maximally, because while someone who had succumbed to temptation might be able to sympathize

with me, "grace to help" can really only come from One who never gave in.

10. Why is granting someone the freedom of choice so crucial in terms of his or her recovery?

11. Discuss the analogy of becoming your heartbroken friend's "birth coach," in terms of both your methods and goals. List as many similarities as you can. How do these compare to the way God "labors" with us?

12. Imagine that the bereaved mother whose nine-year-old daughter's murder is still unsolved is your good friend. It's been two years since the funeral, but she still refuses to change the girl's room. How would you try to help this woman? What choices does she need to make in order to get past the stage she's in? Is her grief, at this point, a coffin or a cocoon?

13. It took Nancy seven *years* to realize and resolve her anger with God for allowing her three-day-old baby to die. Based on your own experience with loss (or trying to help someone else work through theirs), what do you think of this example?

    ❑ Rare—perhaps the circumstances made it worse.
    ❑ Uncommon—but some people do become angry with God.
    ❑ Typical—but mainly because of her religious heritage.
    ❑ Common—most people get angry at God, but repress it.
    ❑ Exemplary—everyone should approach it this way.
    ❑ Other:

Chapter 11

Beauty for ashes

*The deeper the hurt
the more meaningful the healing.*

Dear God,

Do you really cause or allow everything to happen? Sometimes you do something special (like a miracle) for someone. How do you choose who to do that for?

Just what value does prayer have anyway? And what value is there in trying to raise these children for you? We tried, trusted and prayed. *This* is your answer?

After all that happened to Job, couldn't you have said something to him that showed that you understood? Were his children pawns in your test? How could you do that to your faithful servant? Job was one man, one real live hurting person—all that tremendous pain for a lesson to the rest of the world? You allowed (or even caused—you brought Job's name up) all that pain and we are supposed to recognize that you love Job?

It is so difficult to interpret your Word. How do we ever really know just what you mean?

I expected you to hold me. *Where are you?*

Is Angie okay?

Jenny (do you know who I am?)

Jenny's letter to God was her answer to the last question of my survey: "In terms of your own lingering issues with this loss, what question(s) keep coming back into your mind that you might like to ask God?"

After Jenny's daughter, Angie, died of a self-inflicted, apparently accidental gunshot wound (see chapter 5), for a long time Jenny had more questions than answers. But her church friends didn't want Jenny's doubt to hang out: "I was absolutely desperate for people," she wrote. "I needed mature Christians who were able and willing to deal with the issue of pain, to let me question God. I tried bringing up the God issues with Christians I respected, but they simply could/would not deal with it. We must teach our churches to allow people to question God. The statement in your book to 'not fake it or even you will not know when it's real' has helped a lot. If I ever worship God again, it will be with *all* of me."

The Heart of the Matter

The last barrier to recovery is spiritual. The last frontier your heartbroken friend must cross in her journey toward wholeness requires reconciliation with a God who claims to love her, but has at least allowed her to experience heartbreak. Based on years of listening, I believe that one of the most common—though not always verbalized—questions is: *Where were you, God, when I needed you?*

The feelings of abandonment, even betrayal, are often most intense for those who loved God intensely before their loss occurred. So don't be surprised, and don't despair, if your formerly very orthodox friend seems to lose her spiritual bearings for a while.

Your assignment, if you choose to accept it, is to stick as close to her as you possibly can, because her adversary (and yours) is deceitful, crafty, and very experienced in turning perplexity into doubt, and distrust into deep spiritual despondency. The Evil One's goal is, was, and always will be to destroy all the evidence in our world that God is alive, active, and able to redeem even the most painful experiences for his good purposes.

The stakes are very high—even beyond your friend's personal wholeness. For God's method of presenting evidence of his redemptive presence to a skeptical world is, was, and always will be through redeemed people like her; making God visible. Her mission—should she choose to accept it—is to develop deeper faith, for if she does, she'll be able to connect with her broken world far better than a thousand three-point sermons ever will.

The good news in your friend's journey toward resolution is: *The deeper the hurt, the more meaningful the healing can be.* As I've written elsewhere, her capacity for pain is an indicator of her potential for joy. Or, to paraphrase Job's conclusion: "I thought I knew you, God. But that former knowledge was like *hearing about you* versus actually *knowing you personally*."

The only way to get from hearsay faith to eyewitness faith is by asking questions like Job—and Jenny—asked. The harder the better. The questioner's level of openness with God is evidence, not of insolence or heresy, but of relationship. Otherwise, why bother?

Hard Questions

Most heartbroken believers have questions they'd like to ask God:

- "I would like to ask [God] what role he played in ending a beautiful, green-eyed teenager's life," Loretta wrote, after her seventeen-year-old son survived four major surgeries following a motorcycle accident only to die from an undetected blood clot. "I find that after almost nine years, I am *less* able to talk about it! It really depresses me."

- "In Matthew 7:9 you asked, 'Which of you, if his son asks for bread, will give him a stone?'" wrote Sandra, a victim of childhood abuse followed by multiple sclerosis as an adult. "You implied no father would do that—but that's the kind of father I had. I wish you had talked more about *him*, and what to do, how to become whole after having had an unkind father. It would have made it so much more possible to trust you.

  "Also—what do you want me to *do* in this altered body? Did you cause this to happen to me? If so, what for? If you'd just clue me in, I'd go along. Otherwise, it seems like such a waste, and you seem like just another cruel father. Where is the love you promised?"

- "God, how can you take a mom's greatest fear, the death of her child, and mend her heart, allow her to smile again (or) praise you that good things came out of such a tragedy? How do you do it?" asked Wendy, whose twenty-year-old son was struck and killed by an automobile.

Understanding Your Role

If your friend entrusts her hardest questions to you, your first instinct may be to reach for a concordance—or even a multi-volume set of systematic theology—to find a Truth-byte addressing each concern. But to save you a lot of time and agonizing, here's a little secret: *Your friend is not as interested in hearing answers to her questions as you are in providing them.*

You could verify it easily enough by asking: "If I could find the perfect answer to every question you've raised, would you be satisfied?"

Warning: Don't ask this unless *you know for sure* she wants to face the real issues driving her questions. This is very hard to discern. Even when people seem ready, they rarely are. And many cannot handle the idea that they would rather take you in circles than deal with what's really bugging them.

Sometimes people do this when we try to witness to them. The intellectual types, especially, can keep you running for weeks in an effort to refute each of their supposedly sincere objections. But you can discover their spiritual sincerity by asking, "If I could prove to you beyond any reasonable doubt that Jesus is the risen Son of God, would you accept him?"

If they are as sincere as they want you to believe, the answer will be: "Yes, I would," or "I don't know." But only the truly honest will admit, "No, I don't think so." Many times, the real issue blocking a decision to accept Christ is the person's unwillingness to exchange the life he now has for the one God desires for him in Christ.

The core issue for your brokenhearted friend may be similar: *Am I or am I not willing to exchange my brokenness for the ministry God has designed for me?*

No one can make either decision for someone else, and forcing capitulation will only hinder progress toward resolution. So, if your friend isn't ready yet to pursue the exchange in question, don't chastise her for refusing to surrender to God. That's really a highly personal matter between her and him.

Instead, stop and ask the Lord to clarify *what he wants your role to be*—sounding board, encourager, debater, exhorter, what? Very likely, he wants you to be his minister of reconciliation, an ambassador for Christ, appealing to your friend: "I beg you, on Christ's behalf, be reconciled to God." The original words in 2 Corinthians 5:20 are, "as though God were *calling* [appealing] through us." Calling is from the word used to describe the role of the Holy Spirit [*parakaleo*], the One *called alongside*. Your primary role, as one called alongside your friend, is *diplomatic*. Your mission is to be God's agent of redemption in your friend's life.

You can't do this in the ultimate sense that only Jesus could accomplish in terms of salvation as our kinsman-redeemer. But there is a sense in which "redeem" can be applied to recovery from heartbreak. In the midst of one of the most practical discussions of Christian living in the New Testament, Paul says, "Be very careful [literally: *see carefully*], then, how you live [literally: *walk*]— not as unwise but as wise, making the most of every opportunity [literally: *redeeming the time*], because the days are evil. Therefore do not be foolish, but understand what the Lord's will is" (Eph. 5:15-17).

Depending on what stage she's at in processing her pain, your friend may be either *careful* or *careless* about how she's living, specifically which way she's walking in relation to God—toward him or the other way. But if she's ever going to get beyond it, she must come to see her experience wisely, as an opportunity to counteract the fact that the days are evil because the Evil One is bent on destroying her faith and her witness. But there is more to it—as Job's story clearly demonstrates. God, who could have prevented your friend's pain, allowed it because he could foresee how her brokenness would produce the kind of strength, character, and true spirituality that she earnestly desires.

For Reflection or Discussion

1. Why might Jenny's friends have been reluctant to have her bring up "the God issues"?

2. List any "God issues" you have had over the years, and discuss how open you thought your Christian friends were to hearing you out.

3. Evaluate Jenny's statement, "If I ever worship God again, it will be with *all* of me":
    - ❏ As long as she says "if," her attitude is wrong.
    - ❏ The fact that she can even think of worshiping again is positive.
    - ❏ I don't know if *I've ever* worshiped God with all of me.

- ❏ God would be satisfied with any part of her she can offer.
- ❏ With God, it's all or nothing.
- ❏ Other:

4. Why might a person's sense of betrayal by God be greater if his previous love for God was intense?

5. How might the degree of alienation expressed be an indicator of something hopeful?

6. Which of the "hard questions" most fully connected with you? If you were that person's friend, how would you respond?

7. As a group, choose one of the cases and role-play a conversation between that person and her best friend, making sure to include these two components: (1) The hurting person is not as interested in hearing answers to her questions as her friend is in providing them; (2) Because of this, the helper becomes exasperated enough to ask: "If I could find the perfect answer to every question you've raised, would you be satisfied?"

   Debrief, listing any positive or negative principles of helping that can be derived from the role play. After focusing only on that interchange, add any other principles that come to mind from the chapter or from your own experience.

8. If your main role is to be Christ's ambassador to your heartbroken friend, what message have you been asked to deliver? How does your role impact your methods, choice of words, responses, etc.? Use 2 Corinthians 5:11-6:1 to guide your discussion.

9. List the parallel issues in:

    Exchanging your unregenerate life for the one God has called you to in Christ. . . .

    Exchanging your brokenness for the ministry God has designed for you. . . .

    As a group, discuss any surprises when you combine your lists. What is the issue most often involved? How can you help a broken person resolve this issue?

10. Is it proper to think of yourself as God's agent of redemption as you help your friend recover?
    - ❏ Of course not, only he is the Redeemer.
    - ❏ Rather egotistical.
    - ❏ It's her problem; she has to save herself from it.
    - ❏ A good goal, but an awesome responsibility.
    - ❏ Is this another trick question?

11. If it weren't for a sense of God's calling on your life, where would you be? What value has there been in pursuing his way rather than your own?

12. Use this space to write a thank-you note to God for this expression of his grace:

Chapter 12

Seven habits of highly effective comforters

Become a pathfinder through the wilderness of heartbreak.

Next to the Bible, the one book that has most impacted my thinking is *The 7 Habits of Highly Effective People*, by Stephen R. Covey, which describes a multi-faceted model for creating the most effective personal and corporate relationships.

With a tip of the hat to Dr. Covey—and apologies for the comparative superficiality of what I'm about to do with some of his concepts, I want to take one more look at our subject, with a view toward what can happen as you try to help your heartbroken friend.

Habit #1: Be Proactive

When you first discover your friend is facing something devastating, take the initiative *to go to her* rather than waiting for her to call or in some other way ask for help. One of the questions on my survey was "Based on your experience, how do you try to help someone you know is brokenhearted?" A common theme was: "Be there, be there, be there."

There is no substitute. A phone call or letter or especially a telegram will communicate your concern. But in retrospect what your friend will remember is who came. Who stayed. Who cared enough to meet her, person to person, and actually share her pain when the crisis was the most intense.

You don't have to say much. A hug, some tears, and a few words can communicate volumes. After the diagnosis of our second son's illness, my brother, Paul, came over immediately. When I opened the door, he said more *in two words* than some people said during the whole ordeal. "Oh, Dave," he said, as he reached out to embrace me. All we had to do was look into each other's eyes, share the hurt, and be thankful we had each other.

People in crisis will normally be reluctant to ask *anyone* to come, unless they become totally desperate (or know for sure the person in question will *lighten their load*). This is not antisocial. Because what's going on already has drained their energy and threatens their equilibrium, they can't deal with another obligation (beyond survival), including having to explain, converse or in some other way *give* to whoever shows up. So only rarely will heartbroken people call for help, even when many people have said, "Call if you need anything."

However, if you ever do get a call, consider it an S.O.S. Drop everything and get there fast. The only stops you should make are at an ATM to get some cash to put in the homemade card you're going to leave with your friend, and a pizza place, sub shop, or donut stand—depending on the hour, and your friend's favorite food.

On your way, pray. That's as spiritually proactive as you can get. Become your friend's advocate before the throne of grace. When you get there, communicate this message: *We're in this together. We may not be able to control the situation or change what's taken place, but together we will find a way through it.*

Now, about that card. No pretty store-bought card can accomplish what your own words can if you ask the Spirit of God for a creative way to express the love you feel. So, what I'm suggesting you do is make a word-gift to leave with your friend.

What to say? Here are several examples from the final meeting of our group, when I asked the participants to bring a word gift for the person whose name they had drawn the previous week:

> Katherine's read: "My gift to you would be an internal hug you would feel continuously. It would be a sense of security and warmth, that would make you feel competent and loved."
>
> Billy's: "I would give you everything the locusts have eaten, plus a double measure of God's Spirit to enable you to minister his healing to your fellow pilgrims."
>
> To Misty: "Complete joy. God's deep, satisfying joy. Joy in living, joy in loving, joy in giving, joy in being. Then, joy in seeing your dreams come true."

You don't have to be a poet or writer to give your friend a gift like this, since, "A word aptly spoken is like apples of gold in settings of silver" (Prov. 25:11). The main prerequisite is envisioning how he or she is feeling at this moment, and then trying to fill that hole with your love. But if you will engage in proactive inventiveness like this, you have already begun to fulfill the next habit.

Habit #2: Begin with the End in Mind

If you could project yourself to the end of the next twelve months, what would you need to see in your friend's journey through heartbreak in order for you to feel you had been a successful helper? Secondarily, what would you need to see within yourself as a result of your journey with her in order for you to feel the Lord had accomplished all he had in mind *for you* in this experience?

The most effective helpers have a clear sense of mission, whether it be what they are trying to accomplish or what God would like to accomplish through them. This is a difficult, though not impossible, assignment in relation to something as personal as heartbreak, because it's tempting to think in terms of helping people think, speak, or act in some theologically correct manner. *But the core issue of recovery has to do with being, not doing.* With that in mind, just for a moment, pause, close your eyes, and visualize a conversation between yourself and this friend a year from now:

> Where are you? Is it day or night, outdoors or indoors, in a public place or a quiet hideaway? What are you talking about? What kind of words are being used—especially their emotional content? Do you feel free, driven, or constrained in some way? Is your friend at peace, anxious, upset, or angry? Are you better friends in this future interchange than you are today? How are you both different from the way you were?
>
> Now, how do you plan to get from where you are right now—say, driving to the hospital to be with her at the bedside of her mother who has just had a heart

attack and is not expected to live through the night—to where you would like to help her be a year from now?

Of course, I hope you'll keep in mind all the things we've talked about in this book, including being sensitive and patient with her through the first few months. But at some point, she'll be ready to move ahead because she doesn't want to stay where she is anymore. Will you be ready to help her capitalize on this change, and especially to help her move in a constructive direction?

Some of her other friends will push her—at least that's the way it will feel to her. But for every push, there's at least an unconscious resistance, because we don't really know if we can, or should, implicitly trust people who try to force us in *any direction*, regardless of how wholesome and good it may appear to be, to them or to us.

The reason you'll be able to help is because you've been walking beside her, listening, sharing, and caring. But at some point it will be time to lead. The key question, therefore, is, "Do you know where you're going?" This is where the visualization we started this section with comes in. For Christian helpers, the underlying issue is, "Where is God going in my friend's life (and in our experience together)?"

For each person you try to help, the answer will be unique, but the main objective will be the same. Where God is going in every believer's life is found in Romans 8:28-29: "And we know that God causes all things to work together for good to those who love God, to those who are called according to His purpose. For whom He foreknew, He also predestined to become conformed to the image of His Son, that He might be the first-born among many brethren" (NASB).

If you both love God, then you *both* are "called according to his purpose." This means you have a calling or mission. The way out of heartbreak's wilderness starts at the point where this truth is internalized, becoming the central guiding principle around which all else can be arranged. God is able—because he is greater—to cause *anything* to work for good, regardless of how it feels to us at any given moment. Will you dedicate yourself to helping your friend choose to cooperate with him toward that end? The answer will depend on just how focused you can become (and remain) on the most important things.

Habit #3: Put First Things First

In the Christian life in general, people fail to accomplish all they could for God not only because they don't know what they're trying to accomplish, but because they allow the good to distract them from the better, and the better to deter them from the best.

You don't necessarily have to like climbing down in that pit with Charlie (remember chapter 5). The decisive factor is that your purpose to help him out of that pit is given precedence over the degree of your dislike for the way Charlie's problems put a damper on your personal enjoyment of life. In other words, for the joy set before you—his wholeness—you have laid aside certain of your rights to become his servant in the process, regardless of how long it takes. As a friend of mine used to say, "A servant is a person who delights in making another person successful."

Earlier in this chapter, I asked you to visualize what your friend's successful recovery would look like. Now, as you think about helping "Charlie" move toward that goal, the question has become, *What one thing could you do this week (or month) with Charlie that would most likely have a long-term positive impact on his recovery?*

Instead of focusing on Charlie's problems—although you may need to let him keep telling you about them until he tires of hearing his own repetition—focus instead on that one thing and how you can facilitate its occurrence. If you don't, Charlie's problems could lead you both down a bunch of fruitless rabbit trails, and a year from now you'll be right where you are, wondering why.

To help you get started, let's think about what *category* of activity would be most helpful to your heartbroken friend. The best answer, I predict, lies in any direction that would increase his ability to help himself. Ultimately you are not striving for a dependent relationship, but interdependence. When this is over, you want to be functioning side-by-side in the body of Christ, each fulfilling the role God chose for you, long before the loss that brought you together in your present mutually therapeutic relationship.

As you lead your friend in that direction, there will be times when you must say no to some things in order to say yes to others. For instance, in order to maintain your identity while encouraging your friend to take responsibility for his problems, you may have to fight his attempts to draw you in, even absorb you, in issues that are totally his own.

The most significant example of this is his relationship with God, where at the very core of things nobody else can be either his buffer or his scapegoat. He may have to wrestle it out, like Jacob and the angel, and as an observer, you may have to fight your inclination to intervene, protect, or even referee.

But the ultimate reason you'll stay out of it is because when you put first things first, Charlie's need for reconciliation with

God takes precedence over your fear that he might turn away from God, instead. (If he does, you can still walk beside him until he's ready to turn back.)

To take this one step further, Charlie's need for reconciliation with God is really the number-one priority of your journey with him through heartbreak and beyond, because until he has come to a place of loving God, *nothing else will ever really fit as he tries to put the pieces of his life back together.*

As long as at the center there is alienation, fragmentation, or destructive energy of any sort, any recovery Charlie makes will be only partial and temporary.

A few years ago, J. Grant Howard published an insightful and challenging book, *Balancing Life's Demands*, in which he demonstrated that the priority system frequently used by modem Christians is not aligned with what Jesus said. You've heard the list: God, family, church, work, witness, and finally, yourself. By contrast, Jesus said that the whole of divine revelation before his coming could be summarized in the commands to love God with all your heart, soul, mind, and strength and your neighbor as yourself.

Dr. Howard proposed another model with God at the center, and everything else related to him, like parts of a wheel. In other words, the question of priorities is really a question of relationships and responsibilities that all connect at the center with God.

Therefore, if you want to help Charlie reorganize his life, the primary question becomes not what's first, second, or third, but how does his core relationship with God impact all his other concerns? In order to get him to see this, you're going to have to show him how you've worked this out (or are working it out) yourself. To the degree you succeed, you will create a situation where you both can win.

Habit #4: Think Win-Win

One of the biggest problems with Christian helpers is that their help comes with strings attached—usually the person's alignment with a particular viewpoint or dogma. This less than subtle message has more to do with conformity than with mutual discovery of what God is trying to teach both helper and friend through the experience.

Anyone who pressures a hurting friend in this way is repeating the error of Job's comforters, who tried to force Job's grief through the matrix of "good things happen to good people." Today's theologies are more sophisticated, but no less coercive. But, as one of my respondents pointed out, God is not religious. His viewpoint is so far above and beyond anybody's system that we do him a grave injustice when we force him, or *people who are trying to find him*—precisely your friend's problem—through any religion's grid. The only way to a therapeutic relationship where both can benefit, therefore, is to agree with C. S. Lewis's analysis in *The Chronicles of Narnia*, "Aslan [Jesus] is not a tame lion."

If you want to approach helping by asking, "How can we both win?" you must lay aside any agenda that might prevent you and your heartbroken friend from gaining significantly from the journey you've undertaken together. You need to communicate: I'm not the expert, here to give you the goods. Nor do you have to capitulate to anybody's party line. I'm just your fellow pilgrim in a process of discovery about who God is and how he is working in our world today; specifically, in and through the painful experience that has brought us together.

Your heartbroken friend will never fully trust you as long as you have any other agenda in mind except her wholeness

> God is not religious. His viewpoint is so far above and beyond anybody's system that we do him a grave injustice when we force him, or people who are trying to find him— *precisely your friend's problem—through any religion's grid.*

before God. In order to prove worthy of this trust, you may have to protect your friend from all assaults on her integrity by the religious among us who offer affirmation in return for spouting the party line.

Win/win lies in another direction, in giving yourself completely to your friend, regardless of what her response may be. Dr. Covey quotes Dag Hammarskjold, past Secretary-General of the United Nations: "It is more noble to give yourself completely for one individual than to labor diligently for the salvation of the masses."

If you will consciously choose, every time a choice is necessary, for your friend and against the masses, you may become the target of some pious person's reproach. But you and your friend will both win, in the end, because what will happen as you walk together is that both of you will begin to see each new challenge, whether from without or within, as an opportunity in disguise. This is what seeing life with the eyes of faith is all about. But it can only happen if your eyes are open, not shut, to the hidden benefits of facing adversity.

Remember the situation where Elisha and Gehazi, his servant, were surrounded by the enemy and Gehazi said, "Oh, my lord, what shall we do?" Elisha's response was to offer encouragement: "Don't be afraid. . . . Those who are with us are more than those who are with them." Then the prophet prayed, "O LORD, open his eyes so he may see." When Gehazi took another look at the enormous problem, he saw instead that the hills were "full of horses and chariots of fire all around Elisha" (2 Kings 6:15-17).

If you stick with your friend faithfully enough, you may be privileged to have the role of Elisha in her life. But in order to fulfill it, you will have to listen to your friend's concerns and try to understand and share them, before offering *any* solution, spiritual or otherwise. Following the prophet's example, don't chastise your friend for having less than adequate faith. But try to understand the concern, encourage her, and then pray that God would help her comprehend the realities of the situation you're both trying to see more clearly.

Habit #5: Seek First to Understand, Then to Be Understood

In general, helpers spend far too much time talking and not enough listening. Their help, therefore, is often irrelevant because it fails to connect with the friend's real need. There is simply no way around finding the open door of need and entering your friend's brokenness through that avenue, as opposed to "dealing with it" in some prepackaged format.

Dr. Covey opens his chapter on this habit with an illustration that provides an excellent transition between Gehazi's problem and God's solution (my application, not Covey's):

> Suppose you've been having trouble with your eyes and you decide to go to an optometrist for help. After briefly listening to your complaint, he takes off his

glasses and hands them to you.

"Put these on," he says. "I've worn this pair of glasses for ten years now and they've really helped me. I have an extra pair at home; you can wear these."

So you put them on, but it only makes the problem worse.

"This is terrible!" you exclaim. "I can't see a thing!"

"Well, what's wrong?" he asks. "They work great for me. Try harder."

"I am trying," you insist. "Everything is a blur."

"Well, what's the matter with you? Think positively."

"Okay. I positively can't see a thing."

"Boy, are you ungrateful!" he chides. "And after all I've done to help you!"[2]

You wouldn't bother to go back to a doctor like that, yet this is exactly the treatment your heartbroken friend has received from many people who have tried to help: Without any diagnostic workup, your friend has been handed glasses that work for somebody else. Depending on the group, those glasses may work for *everybody* else. Regardless, they *don't* (and really *can't*) work for the one who is having trouble trying to see what God is doing, or where God is going, in his life.

In Gehazi's case, although Elisha wanted his servant to see with spiritual eyes, even the great prophet couldn't make it happen. All he could do was pray, because it was really up to God to correct Gehazi's visual acuity. Once that happened, Gehazi saw the horses and chariots of fire. Interestingly, it doesn't say Gehazi saw exactly the same thing as Elisha, who maybe even saw the warriors in the chariots.

No two people can have the same vision of spiritual realities, after all. There will be similarities—search the Scriptures for yourself sometime, comparing the visions God gave to the prophets. In fact, there *must* be differences in both content and meaning in each case, because the communication of God as interpreted by the Holy Spirit to the heart and mind of each believer is uniquely suited to that person's position on his journey of faith.

So, you need to find ways to keep asking your friend what God is showing or telling him, or what God has been teaching. There are as many ways to do this as there are people, but you must avoid one thing—asking rhetorical questions whose sole purpose is to provide you an opportunity to make your own point. Your integrity as a friend is at stake in the way you handle this. To the degree that you help your friend share what God has been communicating to him, you will progress together toward the next step, communion (or in Covey's terminology: synergy).

Habit #6: Synergize

"Simply defined, it [synergy] means that the whole is greater than the sum of its parts," Dr. Covey states. "It means that the relationship which the parts have to each other is a part in and of itself. It is not only a part, but the most catalytic, the most empowering, the most unifying, and the most exciting part."

He goes on to describe the creative process involved in this as "terrifying . . . because you don't know exactly what's going to happen or where it is going to lead. You don't know what new dangers and challenges you'll find.

"Without doubt," he adds, "you have to leave the comfort zone of base camp and confront an entirely new and unknown wilderness. You become a trailblazer, a pathfinder. You open new possibilities, new territories, new continents, so that others can follow."[3]

This is the way for any relationship (business, home, church, politics) to become the most meaningful and productive for all parties involved. But in our context, perhaps the most significant application has to do with helping your friend (and yourself, as well) learn to trust God. From the moment you first gaze out over that uncharted wilderness of heartbreak—knowing you need to help your friend cross it—to the times you're camped out together in the midst of that wasteland, surrounded by wild animals and other threatening forces, you may often wonder if you have made some grave error in judgment to have started this journey in the first place. You certainly don't feel much like a pathfinder at times like that.

Thankfully, as Covey points out, when synergy is operating, "the whole is greater than the sum of its parts. One plus one equals three or more." Human synergy is a remarkable thing. We need each other. We draw upon each other. We can help each other, as we share this journey we call life. But how much more encouraging it is to know that as believers traverse the wilderness, one plus one *always* equals three because the Lord will never leave us or forsake us.

The biblical passage that perhaps best summarizes this is Ecclesiastes 4:9-12:

> Two are better than one, because they have a good return for their work:
> If one falls down, his friend can help him up.
> But pity the man who falls and has no one to help him up!

> Also, if two lie down together, they will keep warm.
> But how can one keep warm alone?
> Though one may be overpowered, two can defend themselves.
> A cord of three strands is not quickly broken.

In this case, the three-stranded cord is you, your friend, and God!

As you journey with your friend through the wasteland called brokenness, you can go together where neither of you would have the security or courage to go alone, because what you are together is more than either of you could possibly be alone.

And as you go, a curious thing can happen. Instead of always being exhausted from constantly giving and never receiving, you may discover that *through giving you have been receiving*. I know this happened to me when our group was meeting. I'd get home, exhausted from work, not long before the meeting was to start. And even as we got underway, my brain felt fried. But when we finished, an hour and a half (or more) later, after facilitating the sharing of in-sights and concerns, I very often felt energized and renewed.

As you help your friend, there may be moments when the physical, mental, or spiritual depletion is nearly overwhelming, because you have been willing to love her enough to enter and share the pain. It is possible, if you're not careful, that this depletion could take you toward what's commonly called "burnout." But it's not inevitable, as should be obvious when you examine the continual helpfulness of people like Mother Teresa. The key to maintaining, even increasing, your ability to help others is related to the last habit, and perhaps the most important one.

Habit #7: Sharpen the Saw

If you're going to cut down a forest of trees, you need to stop and sharpen your saw when it gets dull—or, if you're wise enough, *before it gets dull*. The same principle applies to helping others recover from loss. Renewal, a lifelong process, is more than a spiritual issue. Just as depletion can involve body, soul, and spirit, renewing those personal resources—or keeping them full—is crucial if you are going to avoid becoming a casualty among many others who have tried to help their friends through brokenness.

Here are a few components of health (see Covey's section on renewal for a more extensive analysis):

- Physical health requires eating right, getting sufficient rest and relaxation, and exercising on a regular basis;

- Emotional health springs from an inner serenity that comes from having resolved the need to prove yourself or make something of yourself. As a result you will be relatively free from anxiety and depression, and conversely relatively happy and satisfied;

- Social health includes open, honest communication with others, with whom you enjoy synergistic rather than adversarial relationships. Because you don't need to elevate yourself at the expense of others, or compete with them to achieve superiority, you are free to accept and affirm others (in other words, treat them with grace) while remaining committed to their best interests as their servant-friend;

- Your mind's health involves reading, reflecting, organizing, and planning, and working hard to communicate your thoughts coherently so that others will be challenged and blessed. Often this includes the "social" aspect of sharpening your thinking in the context of a group, or at least by talking things through with one or more other persons, for "iron sharpens iron," as Proverbs 27:17 says;

- Your spirit's health is, at its core, a function of the depth of your experiential (versus theoretical or primarily intellectual) knowledge of and love for God. This relationship is the key to really living, now and into eternity. The acceptance that comes from God on the basis of your faith in Christ is the reason you have nothing to prove. The renewal of your mind that comes from pursuing Truth, with the Spirit's help, inspires your creative thinking. A deep appreciation for what God has done for you in Christ Jesus drives you to do his will, which is a primary reason you have embraced the ministry of reconciliation in the first place.

These are all factors in the lifelong process of becoming a whole person. Although, in a certain sense, we are whole already, in the mind of God—who sees the perfection of Christ when he looks at Christ's brothers and sisters—there's also a not-yet aspect to the walk of faith. This is one reason we, and our friends, struggle so much with situations that bring us pain. We simply cannot respond supernaturally in every circumstance, because we are not supernatural, nor are we yet perfectly conformed to the image of Jesus.

We long for that day when we will be like him, for we shall see him as he is, but now as we walk this sometimes difficult, confusing and painful path, we occasionally glimpse—as the disciples did on the way to Emmaus that first Easter afternoon—what it will be like to walk and talk with him forever.

If you're like me, you're looking forward to understanding how the things that have so broken me (and my friends) were all tools in the hands of a Divine Sculptor who was chipping away the things in us that didn't look like his Son.

In the meantime, the best we can do is to keep walking, trusting that one day he will make it all clear. As we walk, whether we're trying to help someone else or simply completing the journey set before us, the attitude that will keep us constantly renewed is that of a learner—or to use a synonym—a *disciple*, a student of Christ.

We cannot really help others unless this attitude is our guiding principle. For, as the Teacher once said, "Can a blind man lead a blind man? Will they not both fall into a pit? A student is not above his teacher, but everyone who is fully trained will be like his teacher" (Luke 6:39-40).

As you and I complete the journey represented by this book, I want to make it clear that this disciple is not fully trained, yet, by his Master. But I'm not as blind as I once was, and I do know where some of the pitfalls lie.

My hope is that by internalizing whatever is true, right, honorable, and worthy of emulation in all I've shared—while ignoring the rest—you will be better equipped to complete your own pilgrimage with heartbreak, whether your friend's or your own. I wish, as I come to the end of this book, that I could echo the thoughts of the apostle Paul, "Follow my example, as I follow the example of Christ" (1 Cor. 11:1). But I still feel like I'm in Discipleship 101 at the University of Brokenness, so your best choice will always be to follow Christ. That way, you can't go wrong, nor can you get lost, in your journey toward the wholeness that only knowing him can bring.

For Reflection or Discussion

1. If you learned that your friend's mother was in the ICU as the result of a heart attack and not expected to live through the night, how would you respond "proactively"? Why is this so important?

2. Have you ever been in a stressful situation where you were torn between calling for help and the prospect of having more stress introduced by another person's being around? Describe the experience, focusing on the feelings. How might this impact the way you approach a person with a similar need?

3. Describe the conversation you projected a year from now between your heartbroken friend and yourself. Based on that exercise of imagination, create a group thumbnail sketch of what recovery from heartbreak "looks like."

4. One of the signposts along the way of recovery is when your friend begins to feel he or she doesn't want to stay where he or she is anymore. How could you tell your friend has reached this point? What would you do to capitalize on this change, and especially to help him or her move in a constructive direction?

5. List the differences between pushing and leading someone on the path toward wholeness.

6. Contrast helping relationships that foster dependence, independence, and interdependence. List the characteristics of each, and then discuss how helping styles sometimes have to be flexible, based on the needs of the heartbroken person.

7. Why is it sometimes hard to simply observe while our friends engage in the inevitable wrestling match with God that comes with recovery from loss?
    - ❏ I wish I could protect them.
    - ❏ I fear for their spiritual safety.
    - ❏ It reminds me too much of my own unresolved issues.
    - ❏ It's frustrating, when I know how my friend should choose.
    - ❏ I'm not sure it is inevitable.
8. Can theologies (or denominational dogma) be coercive to people in pain? If you sensed this happening to someone you were trying to help, how would you handle it? If several people in your group have experienced pressure of this sort, have them do a role play, and then discuss it together, especially focusing on how to creatively manage the different forces at work.
9. What agendas might prevent your friend (and you) from discovering through your shared journey all the lessons that God has in mind?
10. How is the hypothetical visit to the optometrist, in which the doctor hands the patient his own glasses—because they work for him—similar to the way heartbroken Christians are sometimes treated? Have you ever been treated in this way? If so, how did it feel? How helpful was the advice (treatment) you received? What might you have said in response? What guiding principle can you see here in terms of how to help somebody else?
11. Mutual discovery of what God is revealing is a major

theme of this final chapter. How does asking rhetorical questions hinder this process?

12. Dr. Covey says that pathfinders or trailblazers must leave the security of base camp to confront an entirely new and unknown wilderness. What parallels can you think of in terms of the challenges of helping a heartbroken friend? Despite the difficulties of this approach, what are the potential benefits—to both you and your friend?

13. Discuss and further develop your own list of components of health. Rate yourself, in each category; then write out a personal improvement plan for the next one month, six months, and one year. Share as much or as little of this exercise as you wish with your group.

14. If you sometimes struggle with the tension between the "already" and the "not yet" aspects of faith, share how you try to approach this. What impact does this tension have on the degree to which we struggle with heartbreak—our own or someone else's? Is there a hidden benefit to this struggle, even though it does represent human weakness?

15. Compare the components of love from 1 Corinthians 13:4-8 with "the seven habits" of highly effective comforters as described in this chapter. What would you add, change, or delete on the list of habits? What areas do you need most to work on, and what specifically do you intend to do in each?

16. If you've been working through this study in a group setting, take a few moments at the end of your final session to give a "word gift" to another member of your group, especially designed to address some need that person has expressed. You can do this verbally, but it might be less

embarrassing and it might avoid the possibility of someone's being left out, if you use the "card" method instead.

Have each member of the group write his or her name on the front of a three-by-five card at the beginning of the meeting, after which these are placed in a container and redistributed, one card to each, so that each participant has one person to think about and give a gift to (by writing it on the reverse side of the card) by the end of the meeting. (Anyone who draws his or her own name should take another card.)

Collect the completed cards, then distribute them by name, and have the recipient read what has been written. Then close with prayer.

Note: You can expedite this process, if your group is the same each week, by distributing the cards a week in advance.

Notes

Chapter Eight: Somebody to Hold Me

[1] George Nichols, "It's Not Hard to Prevent Suicide," *Journal of the Christian Medical and Dental Society*, vol. XXI, no. 1, (Spring 1990), 10-12. Used by permission.

Chapter Nine: To Tell the Truth

[1] Erwin P. Rudolph, *John Bunyan and Pilgrim's Progress* (Wheaton: Victor Books, 1977), 63.

[2] Ibid., 62.

Chapter Twelve: Seven Habits of Highly Effective Comforters

[1] Stephen R. Covey, *The 7 Habits of Highly Effective People* (New York: Simon & Schuster, 1989), 201.

[2] Ibid., 262-263.

[3] Ibid., 263.

About the Author

Dr. David B. Biebel is a minister, author, editor, and publisher. He holds the Doctor of Ministry degree in Personal Wholeness (with distinction) from Gordon-Conwell Theological Seminary in South Hamilton, Massachusetts. Over a period of more than 20 years of his career, he edited two national magazines for Christian doctors; first, the **Physician** magazine for Focus on the Family, and then **Today's Christian Doctor** for the Christian Medical & Dental Associations.

Biebel has authored or co-authored nineteen books, including the Gold Medallion winner **New Light on Depression** and one bestseller: **If God Is So Good, Why Do I Hurt So Bad**, which was recently revised and re-released, with questions for personal or group study. His first book, **Jonathan You Left Too Soon**, considered a classic in the field, was also recently revised and re-released by Healthy Life Press.

Dr. Biebel founded Healthy Life Press (www.healthylifepress.com) to help new authors get their works to market in a variety of formats.

Jonathan, You Left Too Soon
(2015 Edition)
by David B. Biebel, DMin

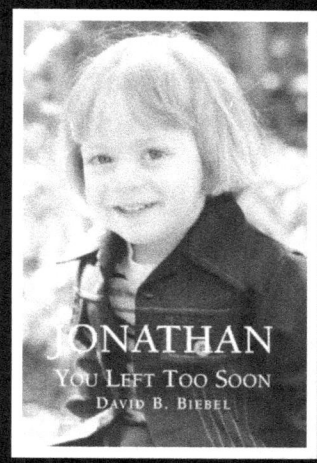

One pastor's journey through the loss of his son, into the darkness of depression, and back into the light of joy again, emerging with a renewed sense of mission. This edition is revised and updated from the classic first published in 1981.

From the Foreword: *Not since Joe Bayly's* A View from the Hearse *have I found myself more in agreement. To this author, grief is real; it dare not be denied or ignored. Yes, its wounds must be handled with care and given time to heal. Preserving us from pious platitudes and empty clichés, David Biebel says it straight and he says it well. Best of all, he doesn't attempt to answer all the whys.*

– Charles Swindoll

Paperback: $14.99   eBook: $4.99
Both: $17.99 (direct from publisher)

More books from the same author

If God is So Good, Why Do I Hurt So Bad? (25th Anniversary Edition)
by David B. Biebel, DMin

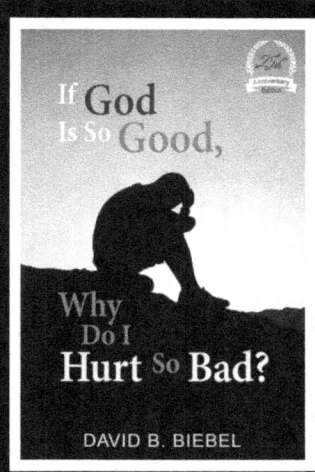

This **25th Anniversary Edition** of a best-selling classic (over 200,000 copies in print worldwide, in a dozen languages) is the book's first major revision since its initial release in 1989. This new version features additional original material related to the conundrum of suffering and faith (with principles learned along the way), and chapter ending questions for personal or group use.

Endorser Sheila Walsh wrote, "*I believe this is one of the most profound, empathetic and beautiful books ever written on the subject of suffering and loss. There is no attempt to quickly ease our pain but rather, with an understanding born in the crucible God uniquely designed for him, David offers a place to stand, a place to fall and a place to rise again. This book left an indelible mark on my heart over twenty years ago and now with this new release the gift is fresh and fragrant. I highly commend this to you!*"

Paperback: $14.99   eBook: $4.99
Both: $17.99 (direct from publisher)

Healthy Life Press

Books, eBooks, DVDs
Golden, Colorado

A Small, Independent Christian Publisher with a big mission—to help people live healthier lives physically, emotionally, spiritually, and relationally.

For a downloadable PDF catalog of our resources, and access to free sample excerpts from our books, visit: *www.healthylifepress.com*

1-877-331-2766 | *info@healthylifepress.com*

www.ingramcontent.com/pod-product-compliance
Lightning Source LLC
Chambersburg PA
CBHW071613080526
44588CB00010B/1119